HEALTHY MEAL PREP FOR BEGINNERS

A Meal Prep Cookbook for Beginners, including Healthy Meal Prep for Weight Loss. Form New Habits to Stop Binge Eating and Emotional Eating

By Suzanne Cook

Text Copyright © Suzanne Cook

All rights reserved. No part of this guide may be reproduced in any form without permission in writing from the publisher except in the case of brief quotations embodied in critical articles or reviews.

Legal & Disclaimer

The information contained in this book and its contents is not designed to replace or take the place of any form of medical or professional advice; and is not meant to replace the need for independent medical, financial, legal or other professional advice or services, as may be required. The content and information in this book have been provided for educational and entertainment purposes only.

The content and information contained in this book has been compiled from sources deemed reliable, and it is accurate to the best of the Author's knowledge, information and belief. However, the Author cannot guarantee its accuracy and validity and cannot be held liable for any errors and/or omissions. Further, changes are periodically made to this book as and when needed. Where appropriate and/or necessary, you must consult a professional (including but not limited to your doctor, attorney, financial advisor or such other professional advisor) before using any of the suggested remedies, techniques, or information in this book.

Upon using the contents and information contained in this book, you agree to hold harmless the Author from and against any damages, costs, and expenses, including any legal fees potentially resulting from the application of any of the information provided by this book. This disclaimer applies to any loss, damages or injury caused by the use and application, whether directly or indirectly, of any advice or information presented, whether for breach of contract, tort, negligence, personal injury, criminal intent, or under any other cause of action.

You agree to accept all risks of using the information presented inside this book.

You agree that by continuing to read this book, where appropriate and/or necessary, you shall consult a professional (including but not limited to your doctor, attorney, or financial advisor or such other advisor as needed) before using any of the suggested remedies, techniques, or information in this book.

Table of Contents

INTRODUCTION 8

Chapter 1: Advantages of Meal Prepping. 15

Chapter 2: Weight Loss-The Macros and The Micros to Achieve Your Goals 25

Chapter 3: The Importance of Mini Meals 45

Chapter 4: Favorite Food 48

Chapter 5: Favorite Cooking 52

Chapter 6: Keto Best Practices 55

Starting A Ketogenic Diet. 59

Chapter 6: Low-Carb 63

Tips And Tricks For Handling Carb Cravings................... 76

Chapter 8: Ingredients for meal prepping 80

Chapter 9: Meal Prep Recipes 83

Breakfast 83

Scrambled Eggs 83

Breakfast Casserole 83

Vegetable Breakfast Bread 84

Breakfast Muffins 85

Eggs Baked in Avocados 86

Chicken Breakfast Muffins 87

Breakfast Pie 88
Breakfast Stir-fry 89
Breakfast Skillet 90
Breakfast Bowl 91
Breadless Breakfast Sandwich 92
Shrimp and Bacon Breakfast 93
Feta and Asparagus Delight 94
Frittata 95
Sausage Patties 96
Smoked Salmon Breakfast 97
Seasoned Hard-boiled Eggs 98
Eggs and Sausages 99
Mexican Breakfast 100
Lunch 101
Caesar Salad 101
Chicken Lettuce Wraps 102
Pizza Rolls 104
Spinach Stuffed Portobello Mushrooms 105
Albacore Tuna Vinaigrette Salad 107
Chicken Quesadillas 108
Shrimp and Cucumber Salad 110
Turkey Wraps 111
Feta Cucumber Salad 112
Cream of Mushroom Soup 114

Chili Mac 116

Barbecue Chicken Pizza 117

Cobb Salad 119

Tuna Croquettes 120

Tacos 122

Cucumber Soup 123

Dinner 124

Grilled Chicken Wings 124

Slow-roasted Beef 125

Roasted Salmon 127

Easy Baked Chicken 128

Italian Pork Rolls 128

Lemon and Garlic Pork 130

Easy Baked Chicken 131

Lemon Chicken...132

Dessert , Appetizers, Side Dish and Salads 133

Portobello Mushrooms 133

Avocado Fries 134

Mushrooms and Spinach 135

Nutty Breakfast Smoothie 136

Cauliflower Mash 136

Simple Kimchi 137

Chocolate Bombs..138

Roasted Cauliflower 139

Broiled Brussels Sprouts 140

Doughnut 141

Oven-fried Green Beans 142

Pesto 143

Creamy Spinach 144

Bonus Recipes..146

CONCLUSION 157

Introduction

Meal prepping is a good idea, but how do you do it exactly? It involves choosing your meals beforehand, keeping them simple, and setting aside a day where you do most of the work like chopping, roasting, freezing, some cooking, and so on. You'll also be multitasking and storing meal components in the right containers for the fridge and freezer.

Here are the must-know tips:

Pick your Meals (3-5 days ahead of time)
Before shopping and prepping, you'll need to know what your meals that week will be. Depending on what your goals are, you can pick as many meals (breakfast, lunch, and dinner) as you want. If you have specific calorie goals in mind for each day, you will need to know all your snacks, too, if you want to be precise. How many days should you have meal plans for? Some people

start out with just 3 days, but 5 days ahead will get the work week planned. Unless you're freezing your food, 3-5 days is usually the maximum for most meal prep like cooked meat, roasted veggies, etc.

Think Simple
The best meals are simple meals especially when healthy eating is the goal. Simple meals also require simple prep, which makes your life much easier. This way, you don't have to stress about complicated cooking processes, getting a bunch of different ingredients at the store, or feeling overwhelmed about counting up calories and macronutrients. When you think simple, you can make a few different meals from staples like eggs, chicken, and vegetables.

Prep on a Specific Yay
Rather than prep throughout the week, it's much more efficient to pick one day and prep most of your meals then. A lot of people choose Sunday, but whatever day you can free up works. If you're concerned about the amount of work and time prep takes, you can save some of the prep for the middle of the week on an evening when you have time.

Be Ready to Multitask
To speed up the prepping process, get ready to do some multi-tasking. You'll be cooking multiple things at once, and using your oven, stovetop, slow cooker, and any other equipment you have, like a pressure cooker. You can cook multiple things in the oven that have similar temperature and time requirements. Writing out the times, temperatures, and cooking method of what you're making can help you stay organized.

When meal prepping, you should pick your meals 3-5 days in advance, choose simple recipes, prep on a specific day, and learn to multitask.

Have the Right Containers
A common refrain of meal-prep articles and blogs is that the right containers are essential to productive meal-prepping. If your food isn't stored properly, it can go bad, dry out, get freezer-burn, and so on. Containers are so important that in the next section, we're going to take the time to break down what makes a container the right one.
What should you look for when selecting a set of containers for prepping? There are seemingly-countless options, and it can get really overwhelming. Here's a list of what you should remember:
Go with Airtight and Leak-proof Lids
This seems like a give-in, but not all lids are created equal. Snap-on lids are common, but they don't always work, so you should test them in-store and not order online if you want to be sure. Look for lids with a good seal and good suction, or with a physical locking mechanism that really keeps the lid shut. Check out reviews and see what people are saying about the lids.

Make Sure the Containers are Microwave-safe
You might think you don't need microwave-safe containers, but they're really useful for heating up leftovers. It also means you can put a whole meal in a container and just grab it when you're going out the door. No extra plates or bowls necessary. If your container isn't microwave-safe, it can warp and melt. It also isn't safe, because materials can leach into your food. You want FDA-approved, microwave-safe containers and lids. If you're still worried, look for BPA-free containers, too. Food-grade silicone

containers are popular for this reason, while glass containers are automatically microwave-safe and free from chemicals.

Get Freezer-friendly Containers
For certain food, you will want to freeze it to make it last longer. Not every container is freezer-friendly, and using one results in food that gets dried out and coated in freezer burn. Look for labels that say the container is okay for use in the freezer, and while glass can go in there, be sure to give your food room to expand. You don't want a cracked container. Gallon freezer bags are always a good option, too.

Get some Portable Containers
Portable containers are awesome since you can take your meals with you. Containers come in a vast variety of shapes and sizes, so think about what you'll be storing and choose accordingly. Chopped veggies and fruit don't need a lot of space, while full meals will need slightly-bigger containers. While we're talking about size, you also want to think about how much room you have in your cupboards for containers you aren't currently using. Collapsible ones can be very convenient. Weight also matters - glass is heavier than plastic, and most people don't find them convenient for traveling.

Make Sure the Container is Durable
You don't want cheap containers that break immediately if you drop them. If you get ones that are microwave, freezer, and dishwasher-friendly, then they are probably durable enough. Always check out the reviews before purchasing. When it comes to the glass versus plastic debate, glass containers aren't fragile - they're made from thick glass - but they are by nature a bit more breakable than plastic.

Think about Cleaning
You'll be cleaning a lot of containers, so how easy they are to get clean and smell-free matters. Plastic containers, even the dishwasher-safe containers, tend to cling to smells. They also will stain at some point and you'll probably want to replace them when they get too gross. Glass containers are much easier to clean and they don't hold on to odors or stains. The same goes for stainless-steel containers, though remember you can't use abrasive sponges or you'll end up with scratches.

Choosing the right containers is essential to good meal prepping, so pick ones that are safe in the microwave and freezer; airtight and waterproof; easy to clean; and durable.

Be Budget-conscious

Containers can get expensive. Think about what you really need for storage, and if most of your prep will be just fine in gallon freezer bags that you put in the fridge or freezer. Maybe splurge on some nice glass ones for meals you know have staining ingredients like tomato or curry sauce. It can be tempting to get one of those big 40-piece sets that go on sale, and if they have good reviews, good specs, and come from a good brand, go for it! Just make sure you have room for them.

Container materials
- Plastic
- Glass
- Silicone
- Stainless-steel
- Ideas for storage containers

- Reusable sandwich bags
- Silicone pint glasses with lids (for smoothies on-the-go)
- Bento boxes with compartments
- Mason jars

What Foods Can't Be Frozen?

If you want to meal prep longer than 3-5 days in advance, you will have to freeze your ingredients or meals you've prepared ahead of time. Because most foods can frozen, it's actually easier to list what foods don't freeze well:

- Yogurt
- Sour cream
- Mayonnaise
- Eggs
- Milk
- Cheese
- Potatoes
- Cream-based soups and sauces
- Fully-cooked pasta
- Salad
- Cucumbers
- Celery
- Spaghetti squash
- Raw peppers
- Zucchini

Take note that the vegetables in the list above do freeze decently when they're in other dishes like casseroles, but on their own, they don't do well. They tend to do better if they're blanched beforehand, but they still don't last long in the freezer.

Chapter 1: Advantages of Meal Prepping

Meal prepping is one of the best ways to feed yourself and your family healthy foods every day. Time is often short when you're dealing with your own schedule and your kid's schedule. Cooking is often a low priority for us.

Meal prepping can help you in a variety of ways, which is what we're going to explore in this chapter. Here are some benefits of meal prepping!

Save Money You'll save money when you eat healthy and prep in advance. The ketogenic diet can be expensive for people who don't buy in bulk, which is where meal prepping comes in handy.

By planning your meals in advance, you're able to buy in bulk which will save you money. You can usually store a meal for at least two weeks in the freezer too. It can help you save money at lunchtime too when you have prepped leftovers.

Weight Loss The ketogenic diet already helps you to lose weight but planning your meals in advance will help you to save a little more cash too. With meal planning, you know exactly how much you're going to eat at a time, which can help to keep you from overeating.

A meal routine will also make it easier to know how many net carbs you're putting in your body each day. You can even label the meals with the amount of net carbs in each one.

Easy Grocery Shopping It's easy to go grocery shopping when you know exactly what you'll be eating and when. Make a list, and just get everything off it. If you are prepping your snacks too, you don't even have to deviate off the list for everything you need.

Just divide your shopping list into different categories like fruits, protein, frozen food, etc., and it'll be easier than ever to avoid aisles where you'd spend too much money or end up straying from the ketogenic diet.

Less Waste Most of the time, you can just eat out of the dish that you've stored your food in. this helps you to cut down on paper plates, plastic utensils, and will keep you from wasting your food if you've prepped in advance. You unitize all the ingredients that you bought during the week, and it helps you to plan accordingly.

Time Saver This is the main reason that people decide to start meal prepping. It's hard to find time to cook three meals a day, but that's exactly what the ketogenic diet requires. By saving time when cooking, you're less likely to eat junk food or fast food too.

Stress Reduction Stress can affect your digestive system, disrupt your sleep and even cause your immune system to suffer. It can be hard to come home from a long day of work and then pan for dinner. With meal prep, you have a dedicated day to get the dinners ready, which allows you to relax most of the time.

How to Start Prepping Today

Let's look at everything you need to start meal prepping today. There are certain ingredients you'll need as well as equipment to get started with.

Meal Prepping Equipment

You'll find essential equipment and what it's used for below.

- Cutting Board: You should try to get boards made from solid materials because they're corrosion resistant and non-porous which makes them easier to clean than wood or bamboo boards. Try plastic, glass, or even marble cutting boards for easier clean up.
- Measuring Cups: It's important that you measure out your spices and condiments accurately.
- Measuring Spoons: Even when you're prepping in bulk, you may still only need a small amount of some spices.

- Glass Bows: Glass bowls are considered easier, but nonmetallic containers will also be needed for storing meat and marinades.
- Packaging Materials: Your non-metallic containers and glass bowls will be important for this as well, but you may also want bento boxes that are freezer safe or even Tupperware. Make sure that you have freezer safe containers too.
- Paper Towels & Kitchen Towels: These will be required for draining meat.
- Knives: Your knives should be sharp to slice meat accordingly. Remember to cut away from your body, and you should wash your knives while cutting different food types
- Kitchen Scale: A kitchen scale can make some recipes much easier, allowing for much more accurate measurements.

• Internal Thermometer: You'll need to check the internal temperature of many meats, especially if you're making snacks like jerky.

• Baking Sheet: This will be needed for many recipes, especially sheet cakes, cookies, or even jerky.

• Colander: You'll have to drain some vegetables and rice.

• Skillets & Pans: It's going to be easier to cook if you have the right sized pan or skillet for what you're doing. You'll need baking dishes too!

Stocking Your Kitchen

While it's impossible to give you a list of each ingredient you'll ever use, there are some basics that you'll want to keep on hand. Before you start prepping for the week, make a comprehensive shopping list according to your meal plan.

• Cupboard Ingredients: Sea Salt, Black Pepper, Tomato Sauce, Tomato Paste, Crushed Tomatoes, Garlic Powder, Onion Powder, Ground Spices, Powdered Sweeteners, Liquid Sweeteners, Canned Vegetables, Almond Flour, Coconut Oil, Coconut Milk, Desiccated Coconut, Nuts & Seeds, Olive Oil, Balsamic Vinegar, White Wine Vinegar.

• Vegetables: Avocado, Onions, Fresh Garlic, Zucchini.

• Fridge: A Pound of Butter, Cream, Yogurt, Eggs, Baby Carrots, Cherry Tomatoes.

Simple Steps for Meal Prep

For whatever day you get started, you're going to want to streamline the process as much as possible. To do that, just follow the simple steps below to help you get started.

Step 1: Make a Shopping List

You'll want to make a shopping list the day before for best results. In the beginning of your 21-day plan, you'll need to make it for a few short days, but at the end, your shopping list will be for a week at a time. Expect to dedicate most of the day to meal prep but remember that it will make life easier.

Step 2: Go Shopping

You'll want to go in and get out when it comes to the grocery store so that you aren't tempted by unhealthy snacks that will pull you out of ketosis. If you have mostly vegetables, try going to the local farmers market where there's less temptation too. A butcher's shop for your meat can also help.

Step 3: Start with a Clean Area

It's going to be easier to start cooking if you clean your area beforehand, and make sure that you have your containers clean too. It's important to make sure you have everything on hand, and it'll help to make it all go by a little quicker.

Step 4: Start Cooking!

Now the only thing left is to start cooking, but make sure that you let your food completely cool before packing it up. If you don't let your food cool, then you can ruin the texture and it may become soggy upon reheating.

Ketogenic diet is not one of those fad diets that you have probably used before, this diet is completely different because it does not put you in a "fast" or "calorie deprivation" mode, rather it works by simply switching your body's mechanism from the usual high carb reliant to a fat-burning mode – this mode makes it easier for your body to build more muscles and cut down fat deposit.

Contrary to the beliefs in some quarters that Low carb Ketogenic diet will cause high fat deposits in the body, due to the presence of low carbs and high protein and fat contents, the reverse is completely the case. The "Low carb" rule here does not mean you have to consume excess saturated fats that cause high cholesterol, it simply allows you to lower your carb supplies enough, and increase other components marginally. The main benefit of Ketogenic diet is that it forces the body to rely on stored fat and fat from diet, as the primary source of energy.

Ketogenic diet helps build more lean muscles while losing fat. The main reason for this is that individuals placed on Ketogenic diets have been found to force their bodies to use up more water, and secondly, the lowered Insulin hormones will force the kidneys to remove excess Sodium and the combined effect of these is that there is a speedy loss of weight within the shortest possible period of time.

Another benefit of Ketogenic diet is that, it targets fat deposit in the most difficult parts of the body, most especially the abdominal region, thighs and the upper chest areas. Starving yourself may not help cut fat in the most difficult regions, even when you lose fat in such areas, they may return quickly, but this is not the case with Ketogenic diets. Losing weight around your mid-section and around vital organs is necessary in order to avoid serious fat-related diseases.

Ketogenic diets increases the amount of HDL cholesterols while reducing LDL cholesterol levels. Choosing the right type of unsaturated fats in your Ketogenic diet will help increase good cholesterols (HDL cholesterols), and these are healthy for the heart and general wellbeing. Ketogenic diets also help regulate blood sugar levels while reducing the risks of insulin intolerance. When carbs are broken down, they release sugar into the blood quickly and this increases blood sugar rapidly, a condition that triggers more supply of Insulin hormones, but when Ketogenic diets replace high carb diets, less sugar are released slowly into the body, a situation that can stabilize the secretion of Insulin hormones.

How does It Help You to Lose Weight?

Ketogenic diet was coined out of the word "Ketosis", a process whereby the body breaks down more fat into fatty acids and ketones. The breakdown of more fats and ketones will provide sufficient energy sources for the body. Free fatty acids and ketones are simultaneously released in into the body during ketogenic breakdown, these are then made available for the body to burn as fuel.

Normally, the body relies on Glucose as the main source of energy, however, glucose is released when the body breaks down carbs, but the bad side of relying on glucose for energy is that, it can be readily stored as fat in fat cells, organs and tissues, when the energy is not used up. On the other hand, starving the body of glucose will force it to use stored fat in your organs as a source of fuel, even before they are stored for too long inside the body. With the burning of more ketones and fatty acids, there will be less glucose in the body to burn and the body will rapidly adjust to ketogenic phase of deriving energy.

You need to have it in mind that the body can only burn the source of energy present, therefore, constantly consuming ketogenic diet will make fats and proteins readily available as source of energy , as opposed to carbs. Ketogenic diets are effective in two ways, first, they create a net balance of energy in the body , and secondly, they rapidly fill you up (increase satiety), thus, you consume much less than necessary.

With Ketogenic diet, you have to avoid or limit your consumption of carbs to less than 5% of your daily dietary intake. Secondly, you need to avoid unhealthy carbs such as tubers, starches, sugar and other processes foods.

How does Ketogenic Diet Help You Lose Weight?

What your body is designed to eat will definitely affect whether you lose weight or not. The earliest humans often rely on what they get during hunting to survive, these include; edible foods, fish and meat, with little or no starch or carb, and that is one of the reasons why they stay slimmer and healthier. With the discovery of processed foods in the modern world (including pasta, white bread and sugary drinks), our bodies have been re-constructed to adjust to such unhealthy lifestyles.

One problem with most starch and sugar is that they can be converted into simple sugars that can be absorbed readily in the blood stream, and the effect of this is that there is a rapid increase in blood sugar level, a condition that triggers a sharp increase in the secretion of Insulin hormones, and this increases the risk of developing diseases such as diabetes type II through rapid weight gain and obesity.

One problem with carbs and sugars is that they increase your cravings, while Ketogenic diet helps you feel fuller quickly and reduce them. The early men consume more of ketogenic diets, and that is why they consume much less but get more energy for hunting expenditures. Ketogenic diets helps lower your body's reliance on insulin hormones, and then makes it easier for the body to use up its fat reservoir as a source of energy.

You don't have to starve yourself to enjoy the benefits of Ketogenic diet, likewise, there is no need to start counting those calories.

Chapter 2: Weight Loss-The Macros and The Micros to Achieve Your Goals

The correct calorie and macronutrient intake effects the most important role in achieving high level physique goals. Tracking our total food intake is the easiest and most reliable way to lose body fat or gain lean body mass

The main purpose behind guide is to help you better understand the relationship between how much and what we eat and the way our bodies look. My hope is that this information will save you a lot of time and effort as well.

What Is Weight Loss

Weight loss is basically weight that you lose when your body undergoes a process of what the experts term as caloric deficiency. This can be achieved either by boosting your calories requirement through building of muscle mass whilst keeping your intake constant, or via calories restriction in the form of a diet where your daily calories intake is designed to be lesser than your daily requirement.

When your body finds itself in a state where calories input is lesser than what it needs for daily function, it will seek to get energy from stores of energy within your body. Most of the time these would be from the stores of glucose found in the liver as well as from your muscle. The other major energy store found in our body would be the fats that we carry on our frame. This is where the tricky part comes in. If your body isn't conditioned for burning fats, it will quickly use up the glucose stores and that is when the feeling of hunger will come in to potentially derail you from your weight loss mission.

Some Common Weight Loss Principles to Note

To help with the process of losing the unwelcome weight from your body, here are some of the more common principles which are good to base your weight loss strategies on.

Keep hunger at bay – Many folks start off on dieting to lose their excess weight and attempt to get healthy but quite a number fail and fall by the wayside. In the end, these folks have to resort to medications and drugs in order to suppress the symptoms and conditions that accompany obesity. It is definitely not a pretty sight, and it sometimes is quite depressing to see people consign themselves to such a fate when more efficient and healthier solutions are actually just around the corner.

They may have started off strong and seen results after some time, but invariably, the one thing that always put paid to these efforts would be the feeling of hunger that many of these diets entail. Take a plain calorie restriction diet plan for example, if your daily requirement works out to be about 1,750 calories, just polishing off a bagel for a snack would set you back by 250 calories. That is like one seventh of your total requirement. Imagine eating seven bagels for the whole day, would that be enough?

The trick of course is to get onto a diet and lifestyle change where you are able to feel full and keep the hunger pangs at bay and yet get your body to lose weight. Know of any diet that does just that?

Be sustainable – There are many ways to lose weight, that is for sure. Getting on the latest fad diet, juicing, fasting, going the vegan way. I have to say as a matter of fact that I hold all these methodologies in high esteem and it is my opinion that each one of them has their benefits for the human body.

Fasting for example, is a good way to let the body rebalance itself and to get rid of toxins that have built up over time. One of the side effects of fasting would be loss of body weight. However, you would not expect a person to fast for a lifetime, without any consumption of food. For any method of efficient weight loss, it must be sustainable in practice to allow for continued shedding of the excess pounds and also to prevent the dreaded bounce back in weight that has plagued so many

One of the benchmarks of sustainability for diets would be the ease of implementing it in everyday life. Imagine if you are on a diet that requires you to eat six to seven small meals a day, you would definitely have to pack for those meals and also find the time to consume them during the work day.

Exercise – Regarded as one of the main pillars for weight loss, exercise, especially strength training, can help to build muscles that burn more calories, not to mention getting you that ripped figure. Yes, it was always good to dream that there was some magic pill in the market that could get you whipped in shape without any effort, but alas, it still remains a dream.

Strength training, done through weights at home or by hitting the gym is one of the surest ways that weight can be lost. Most of the time, it would be advisable to have a schedule for the days that you work out to concentrate on specific muscle groups. This targeted training helps to speed muscle development, leading to higher calorie usage and hence weight loss.

There will be loads of resources online on how to work out a proper strength training routine. The more important thing is to have the discipline to keep plugging at it until you see or feel the results. Believe me, it will be worth it.

First of all, you have to take a look at your diet, the amount of exercise you get per week, how much sleep you get a night, and then use this information to understand how much it will have to change based on your goals.

If you're eating bad every day, going too fast food spots, and only feel your blood pumping when your favorite TV show is about to come on, and you're only sleeping five or six hours a night, of course, you are going to feel bad, and look bad.

Don't worry because you are going to be learning all the process and you are going to be and feel healthier than ever.

You cannot expect your body to be able to look and feel its best when you don't give it the vitamins and nutrients it needs to be vigorous, healthy and attractive looking. There's no magic pill that you can take or some machine that you can put minimal effort into and expect to have abs by dinner time. It takes hard work, and consistency to tell your body it's going to change.

The great thing is your body wants to change; it wants to be healthy, it wants to be free of disease and sickness, it wants you to be proud and able to show it off, you just need to start the process by changing your diet and workout, (or adding an exercise).

Everybody has abs. Some people have long torsos and have six abs; some people have four, some even have eight. We all have them, but not everybody is comfortable proclaiming they have abs because they are covered by layers and layers of fat.

To strip the fat off, you need to expend (burn off/get rid of) more calories than you intake in a day.

It's not necessary to count calories though, and it's a lot simpler if we don't. All we need to do is

eating at regular times in the day, small healthy meals, and have some workout that we follow consistently three or more times a week.

Doing crunch after crunch will not make you get rid of the fat on your stomach. It might burn calories and strengthen your abdominals and make it so that when you are low enough body fat, they will be sharp and beautiful enough to be proud of really, but it's not as efficient as doing cardio, on the treadmill for example.

Don't worry; this is going to be fun! You are going to be healthy, with more energy, and a peaceful mind after reading this book. It is going to be tough, I know. But you are going to love the process, once you achieve your goals.

You are not alone. Many people are striving to be thinner, healthier and have a good quality of life. And many people do it...so I'm pretty sure you will.

Obesity and its Major Causes

According to the American Council on Exercise, to lose one pound of fat, you need to burn a whopping 3,500 calories. Weight loss ultimately comes down to one simple equation: if you eat more calories than you burn, you'll gain weight. If you eat fewer calories than you burn, you'll lose weight. It sounds easy, but it's obviously a lot harder than you'd think. A lot of people have problems trying to lose weight in a healthy way as well, for example they try to stop eating, or eat certain foods that don't have the right nutrients for the body. Weight loss is difficult, especially when it comes to making it a lifestyle that you can sustain.

So how do you know if you're in the danger zone when it comes to a healthy body mass index? To understand this, it's important to know what it exactly means to be obese or overweight. It's crucial to understand that being obese and being overweight mean two different things. Obesity means having excessive body fat that could result in a negative health impact, whereas being overweight means weighing more than what's considered normal, which doesn't have to mean excess fat. An obese person has a BMI (body mass index) of over 30 while an overweight person has a BMI of 25 and 29.9. A normal BMI is around 22. Here, we'll list out some major causes of obesity.

Genetics
According to research, genetics plays an important role in chance of obesity. Part of the cause of obesity can highly depend on the medical history of the individual's family. The risk is two to eight times higher for a person with a family history in obesity as opposed to a person with no family history in obesity.

Lack of Physical Activity
Obesity is normally caused by eating too much and moving too little. Considering real life situations, 70% of jobs involve a minimum of 8 hours/day sitting. That's a LOT of time spent not moving. A study was shown that runners who take part in these job roles actually have side effects from sitting so much. Sedentary activity creates a lot of health problems. Rather than sit the whole day, try to stand up and walk around as much as possible. Try to get at least 1 hour of exercise in per day.

High Intake of Calories
It requires self-control and determination to stop consuming too many calories. Try to only eat when you're hungry. However, don't NOT eat in an unhealthy way. 80% of us tend to leave our stomachs empty for more than 2 hours. Instead of doing this, always try to feed yourself small portions of healthy food every 2

hours a day. This will actually help prevent yourself from having cravings for junk foods like your favorite chips and candy.

Have you ever wondered how many calories you're consuming on a daily basis by drinking your favorite beverages? Sweet, sugary drinks are very high in calorie intake, including orange juice (110 Cal), a medium mocha (400 cal), Coca Cola (280 cal), and sweet tea (200 cal). Consuming alcohol is another unhealthy habit that is costly in terms of calorie intake, e.g. beer is around 150 calories. It seems like everything that tastes good is bad for you, right? We'll get into how to combat cravings and identify healthy food substitutions.

Lack of Sound Sleep

Having a good amount of sleep serves you in numerous ways. It is recommended by experts to have a minimum of seven to eight hours of sleep a day for a healthier lifestyle, with 8 hours a day being optimal sleep.

Now, you should understand what causes unhealthy weight gain.

What are my goals?

Perhaps the most important step of this entire process is establishing exactly what it is that you want to accomplish. It would be a good idea to buy a journal or a notebook and dedicate it purely to this process. Copy your goals into the notebook, and also post them in a prominent place where you will see them every day. Use them as a reminder of what it is you want to accomplish when you feel your routine isn't working, or you're tired, or you don't want to exercise.

Setting goals can be difficult. Luckily, we have a guide to help you through.

Make your goals realistic:
If you're not the kind of person who is going to be a size two don't try and be a size two. I know it's difficult to have a realistic notion of body image when we're constantly bombarded by unhealthy images of emaciated models and stick thin celebrities. But remember, beauty is more encompassing than that. Maybe a better goal is to lose a certain amount of weight per week, or maybe you want to meet a certain weight by your friend's wedding. Those are all good goals to make, just make sure they're realistic for you. Otherwise, you'll be discouraged and can undo any results entirely.

Don't make goals about weight alone:
Don't make your focus weight loss all the time. Maybe you want to run a 5k, or simply start walking to work instead of driving a few blocks. Other ideal goals are to replace one serving of starches with a serving of leafy, green vegetables every day. These goals are all small, manageable, and will ultimately lead to the ultimate goal of weight loss and a healthier you.

Make your goals health oriented, not just about vanity:
Weight-loss is great. Looking killer in those new jeans is great. But what's really great is knowing that you have the energy to keep up with your kids or grandkids. It's knowing that you can go on a hike with a friend without falling behind. Perhaps an ideal goal would be to lower your resting heart rate, or to be able to walk up the stairs without getting winded.

Set goals. Make them realistic, make them creative. Your goals can and should be as diverse as you.

The most important reminder I can offer you in terms of goal setting is to set small goals along the way because that will keep you on track to achieving what it is you want most.

Let's talk about diet, not dieting

Diet is a buzzword most people really don't want to hear. Diet supposedly means restriction; it means confining your life to salads and protein shakes. It makes people feel like they can't even have a life.

Don't believe them. In fact, we're going to change the meaning of the word "diet" right now. Diet simply means what you eat. When people say they're "going on a diet" they mean that they're going to buy in to some ridiculous fad that they will inevitably drop before the pounds even do. When I say the word diet, I just mean the content of what you use to feed yourself. What is your plate made up of? Nobody here is "going on a diet," I promise.

Now, let's talk about food and how we should eat it. First off, your diet is only one part of an overall lifestyle you need to be healthy. Instead of talking about the foods you can't have, I'm going to focus on the foods you should have more of.

Foods you should have more of:

This might be obvious to some. People tend to think they need to eat fruits and vegetables and not a lot more. You are wrong. It's more complicated than that. Here is what you should be eating to stay healthy and drop a little weight:

Green, leafy vegetables: sneak them into a smoothie or a flavorful salad. Keep the iceberg lettuce for the rabbits. You need spinach, kale, and arugula – a complex mix of leafy greens. My favorite thing to do is put them in a smoothie with some berries, bananas, or any fruits you enjoy. It's healthy, delicious, and you can't even taste the greens.

Complex Carbs

Cutting carbs isn't always a great idea. It can leave you low on energy and craving high-carb, high-sugar foods later on. If you start your day with high fiber, complex carbs such as fruits, vegetables, oatmeal, whole grains, or bran cereal, you're far less likely to reach for the candy bar later.

Good Fats

Fats, much like carbs, are foods we need in our diets. They help with brain function and heart health. They also keep you full longer and help to process vital nutrients. Good fats are found in foods such as avocados, olive oil, and nuts.

Do you see what we did here? I did not tell you what foods to cut, I told you what foods to add. As a result of adding those foods, you will automatically cut other, more harmful foods from your diet. Did you know that eating avocado or nuts can help curb chocolate cravings? That's because when you have a craving, it's your body's way of telling you what you need.

How To Meal Prep For a Weight-Loss Diet

Meal prep is essential for success on a weight-loss diet. Always having healthy, low-calorie food available when you need it makes it harder to indulge in temptations or skip meals and fueling snacks. Here are some tips that can make your weight loss journey easier:

Prep Your Snacks

A lot of weight-loss diets will forbid snacks, but the reality is that the "six small meals a day" concept works much better than eating three big meals per day. The six small meals translates into three "main" meals and three small snacks. These snacks ensure you never feel hungry or get low blood sugar, which are both recipes for temptation. Prepping these snacks is important, so you always have something healthy and low-calorie available when you need it. Prep is easy, since you aren't preparing various pieces of a meal. You can just chop up some vegetables with a yogurt-based dip and store it in a container, spread some nut butter on celery, and so on.

Buy Lots of Frozen Vegetables

Vegetables are low-calorie, but high in fiber, which means they make you feel full. You'll be eating a lot of them on a weight-loss diet. Buy lots of frozen veggies, so they'll last longer and you can prepare them really quickly. Frozen veggies have the same nutritional value as fresh.

Take the Time to Prep a Good Breakfast

Breakfast is a very important meal; it jumpstarts the body's metabolism for the day. Take the time to prep healthy recipes like egg muffins in muffin tins, a big batch of steel-cut oats, and so on. If you have the time, it's a good idea to prep 3-4 days in advance, so you don't need to prep your breakfast every night.

Meal prepping for a weight-loss means you should prep all your snacks; buy lots of frozen veggies; always make a good breakfast; and portion everything on prep day.

Portion Everything on Prep Day

When you're prepping your meals on the day you've chosen, portion all your meals and snacks. Since weight-loss diets are calorie-based, you'll be portioning with around 500 cals for breakfast, 500 for lunch, a few hundred for snacks, and the rest for dinner. If you do little else in the way of prep, you should at least portion, because then you know you'll be sticking to the diet the rest of the week and won't have to bother worrying about counting calories all the time.

Aerobic Exercises

Aerobic Exercises are best for Weight Loss. You can do it at home, and you need only 30 minutes in gym for your weight loss regime.

Jumping Ropes

It boosts the heart rate and improves cardiovascular health by strengthening the heart muscles, It improves blood flow through arteries and veins. You need a pair of good sports shoes and a jumping rope. Do it for 3-5 minutes initially, and then increase it to ten minutes.

Nutrients are simply the things that your body gets from food. Your body is much like a car engine. A car needs the right gas, oil, and air intake to run properly. Your body needs the right nutrients to run properly. It also needs the right nutrients to be able to regulate weight effectively. We are going to discuss the 3 macronutrients; carbs, fats, and protein.

Everything in Moderation

There is one rule that we need to look at before we get into the nutrients. It is everything in moderation. As we discuss each nutrient, you will see how fad diets work by creating huge changes in your body. These changes are also why the results don't last very long.

The key is not to cut any one thing out of your diet completely. It is to learn how everything affects your body and then use moderation to control your intake. This helps to ensure that your body is able to work at its peak performance level.

Dieting is more than watching calories. We will be looking at three nutrients in particular; protein, carbohydrates, and fats. Carbohydrates and proteins only have 4 calories per gram and fats have 9 calories per gram. Lifelong weight control success depends on learning about these nutrients and how to eat them properly.

Proteins

Protein is the most important macronutrient while dieting. When protein is digested, it breaks down into amino acids, which are the building blocks of muscle. Amino acid availability is directly proportional to protein synthesis/muscle building. Protein can help maintain muscle while in a caloric deficit because it increases protein synthesis. It can also help build muscle while in a caloric surplus for the same reason.

Carbohydrates

Carbohydrates or "carbs" have gotten a bad name over the last couple of decades. This is largely due to the low carb diet craze. But, if you tried a low carb diet then you found yourself both losing weight and your energy level. That is because of how the body uses carbohydrates.

Carbohydrates are broken down by the body into glucose (sugar). This is the basis for people that advocate a low carb diet. But, this glucose is also what your body uses for energy. If you take it away completely then you rob your body of its energy supply.

Initially, this will yield results. Your body will turn to fat stores for energy. That is why people on the low carb diets lose weight quickly. The problem is that after the fat stores are depleted, your body turns to your muscles. It starts breaking them down for energy.

Fats

Fats are an essential part of our diet. If you were to eat no fat at all then you would actually endanger your health. Of course, on the other end, you don't want to be eating a fatty steak for every meal.

During digestion, fats are broken down into fatty acids. Fatty acids are important for a couple reasons. They are essential for proper regulation of hormones and for caloric manipulation and buffering.

If you are not getting enough fats, then you can experience a hormonal imbalance. It can cause some hormone levels to decrease. This decrease in hormone levels can have adverse effects on your overall health.

You are going to see a pattern here. Fats also can be detrimental to your health in large quantities. Since fats are calorically dense, if you eat too many fats then your body will store the excess as body fat. This is why moderation is in order. You need to strike a balance between eating enough fats to ensure proper hormone function but no so many that your body fat percentage increases. What is the proper balance? This is the million-dollar question. It is also the thing that the majority of people don't know. It is really not that hard. I recommended that you keep your intake of fats between 15% and 30% of your total caloric intake.

You now have a basic understanding of the three macronutrients. This is the start of your journey towards controlling your weight. The next step is understanding how your body uses these nutrients.

Nutrients and Body Composition

Most diet plans take a "one size fits all" approach to weight loss. This is also the reason that most diets do not produce lasting results. We will discuss how to identify your body type and the diet formulas that work best for each body type. The three main body types are:

Ectomorph

This type of body composition shows itself as a skinny person. They have smaller joints and are naturally scrawny. Their limbs tend to be longer and thinner. Their shoulders are thinner and aren't usually very wide.

If you have this body type, then obesity is not usually a problem. In fact, this body type has a hard time gaining weight. Their metabolism runs faster. To be able to gain weight, this body type has to take in large amounts of calories.

A good formula for this person's caloric baseline is their current body weight x 16. This is the number of calories they would have to eat to maintain their current weight.

Keep these formulas in mind when creating your daily diet:

- Protein intake should be 1 to 1.2 grams per pound of bodyweight
- Fat intake should be no more than 25% to 30% of your total calories
- You want the remainder of your calories to come from carbohydrates

Mesomorph

This body type is characterized by bone structure that is larger. Their muscles are more dense and much stronger. This is usually characterized as a more athletic build. This body type usually has an easier time both increasing muscle mass and losing weight.

A formula for this body type to maintain weight is their current body weight x 15. If a person wants to lose weight with this body type, then you want to keep calorie intake under this and vice versa.

When you are creating a daily eating plan for this body type, keep these formulas in mind:

- Protein intake should be 1 to 1.2 grams per current bodyweight
- Fats should make up between 15% to 25% of the total calorie intake
- The remainder of your calories should come from carbohydrates

Endomorphs

This body type struggles to keep fat off. They are generally softer and will gain weight very easily. This is because their metabolism is very slow and cannot burn enough calories. However, this body type builds muscle easily.

To maintain weight, this body type's calorie intake is their current body weight x 14. To lose weight, their calorie intake will need to be less than this.

To lose weight use these formulas for creating a daily diet plan for Endomorphs:

- Protein intake should be 1 to 1.2 grams per current bodyweight
- Fat intake should make up 25% to 30% of your total calories
- The rest of your calories should come from carbohydrates

Fat intake is higher with this body type than the others. This is because it will limit the amount of carbohydrates consumed.

Reaching Your Weight Goals

You now understand how to identify your body type. You also understand the formulas necessary to create your own diet plan. As you can see, this plan is more about the calories and nutrients that you eat instead of the specific food. We have not talked about individual foods. That is because these formulas work with any type of food. The only caveat to this diet is to make sure you are consuming an optimal amount of fiber to keep digestion regular. 15-20 grams per day is sufficient.

Now we are going to look at how to apply these formulas. Once you have the number of calories and macronutrients that you need to take in daily, you can start your diet.

You start your diet plan with these baseline numbers for caloric intake and macronutrients. The next step is to track your progress. If you are not making progress biweekly, then increase or decrease either your fats by 5-10 grams or your carbs by 20-30 grams. Only adjust these numbers if progress begins to plateau. Keep in mind that you don't want to lose more than 1 to 2 pounds per week.

Once you are losing weight at the optimal rate then you have a diet plan that is successful for you. At that point, you only need to continue with these calorie numbers to maintain your new weight. You also will have a plan that will work for the rest of your life.

You can see that we haven't discussed any fad diets. We haven't discussed taking away the foods that you love. Instead, we have looked at the macronutrients that you are getting from food and your calorie balance. This is a plan that is 100% sustainable and doesn't produce the Yo-Yo effect of other diets.

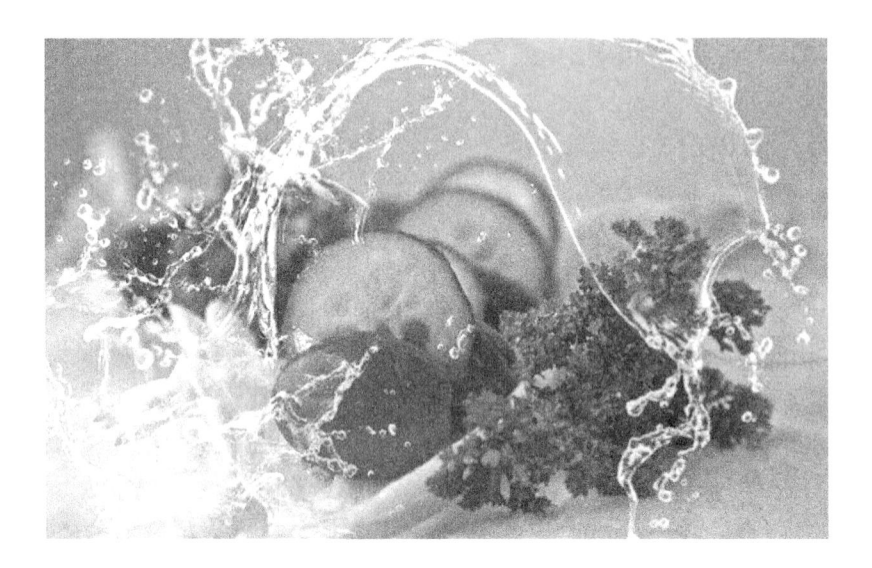

Chapter 3: The Importance of Mini Meals

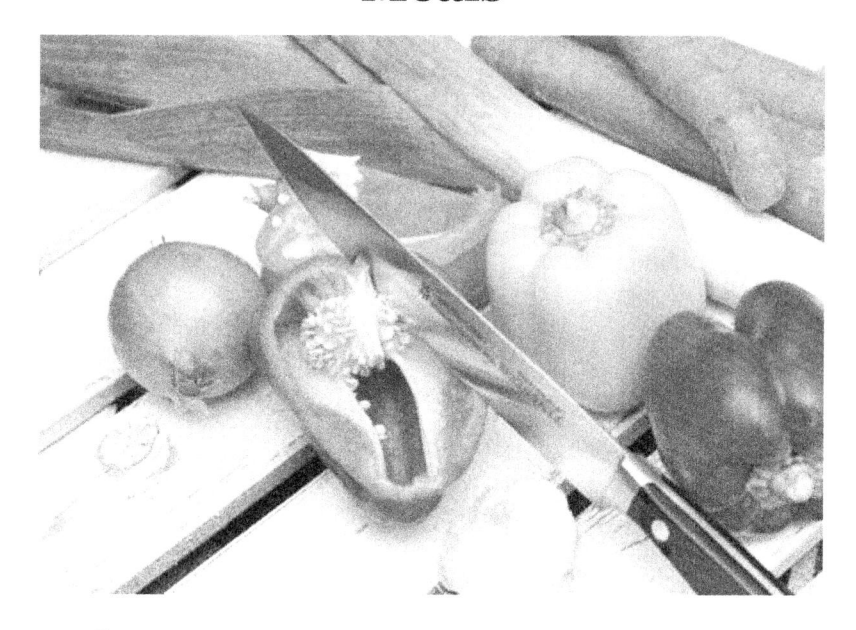

5 Meals a Day

Day 1
Breakfast: Berry Smoothie
•Net Carbs: 8
Lunch: BLT Salad
•Net Carbs: 2
Snack: Green Salmon Bites
•Net Carbs: 5
Dinner: Ginger Soup
•Net Carbs: 5
Dessert: Coconut Macaroons
•Net Carbs: 2
Daily Net Carbs: 22

Day 2
Breakfast: Yogurt Parfait
•Net Carbs: 9
Lunch: BLT Salad
•Net Carbs: 2
Snack: Spinach Dip
•Net Carbs: 4
Dinner: Buttery Garlic Shrimp
•Net Carbs: 4
•Side Dish: Creamed Spinach
o   Net Carbs: 1
Dessert: Chocolate Bacon
•Net Carbs: 0.5
Daily Net Carbs: 20.5

Day 3
Breakfast: Yogurt Parfait
•Net Carbs: 9
Lunch: Fish Curry
•Net Carbs: 4
Snack: Green Salmon Bites
•Net Carbs: 5
Dinner: Ginger Soup
•Net Carbs: 5
Dessert: Banana Fat Bombs
•Net Carbs: 1
Daily Net Carbs: 24

Day 4
Breakfast: Green Smoothie
•Net Carbs: 9
Lunch: BLT Salad

•Net Carbs: 2
Snack: Cheesy Bacon Deviled Eggs
•Net Carbs: 2
Dinner: Herb Pork Chops
•Net Carbs: 0
•Side Dish: Creamed Spinach
   Net Carbs: 1
Dessert: Raspberry Popsicle
•Net Carbs: 8
Daily Net Carbs: 22

Day 5
Breakfast: Yogurt Parfait
•Net Carbs: 9
Lunch: Twisted Tuna Salad
•Net Carbs: 5
Snack: Cheesy Bacon Deviled Eggs
•Net Carbs: 2
Dinner: Buttery Garlic Shrimp
•Net Carbs: 4
•Side Dish: Roasted Radishes
     Net Carbs: 2
Dessert: Vanilla Pudding
•Net Carbs: 2
Daily Net Carbs: 24

Chapter 4: Favorite Food

When people choose vegetarianism, odds are they're doing it for health reasons. By choosing to eat only plants, a person's diet is most likely low in cholesterol, added sugar, and saturated fat. Plants are rich in fiber, minerals, and vitamins, which can reduce risk of illnesses like heart disease, diabetes, and some cancers. However, a vegetarian diet isn't "healthier" by default, especially when you consider how processed a lot of meat-free packaged foods are. A person can also eat a lot of refined grains and sweets and remain "vegetarian," but they won't be very healthy. To make the most of a meat-free diet's health benefits, you need to eat lots of fresh produce and whole grains, while reducing your consumption of processed goods.

How to Eat on a Vegetarian Diet

How do you stay healthy on a plant-based diet? There are four tips that can help you reap the many benefits:

Consider Eating Fish
Before you commit to vegetarianism or veganism, think about adding fish to your diet. Why? Those foods have a lot of nutrients (like the iron in fish and seafood) that can be tricky to replace with vegetables. Pescetarians are less vulnerable to iron-deficiency anemia, which is common for meat-free dieters. Omega-3 fatty acids are also found in their best forms in fish like salmon. If you are hesitant to eat fish for environmental reasons, there are places you can buy from that are cruelty-free and adhere to certain sustainability standards.

Watch Your Iron Levels
Iron is the biggest issue for vegetarians. If you aren't careful, you can become deficient. Symptoms include fatigue, weakness, dizziness, shortness of breath, and headaches. Be sure your diet is full of iron-rich foods like spinach, nuts, pumpkin seeds, collard greens, quinoa, fortified grains, and blackstrap molasses. You should also eat fruits with lots of Vitamin C, because the iron in plants isn't as easily-absorbed as iron from meat. Vitamin C can help with that absorption. If you're still having issues, you might need to consider an iron supplement. Cooking with a cast-iron skillet or a tool like Lucky Fish, a little fish-shaped piece of iron you can boil with broth and acid, enrich your food at home.

Be aware of your protein levels

One of the myths about plant-based diets is that you don't get enough protein. There are lots of really good sources of protein, like eggs, tofu, lentils, beans, nuts, and more, but you should be intentional about choosing the best foods. There is a slight difference between animal and plant proteins, with animal proteins containing more essential amino acids per gram, but you generally eat more of a plant protein anyway because it takes more to feel full. If you struggle with fatigue, joint pain, a slow metabolism, and trouble concentrating, up your intake of protein.

To stay healthy on a vegetarian diet, consider eating fish; watch your iron and protein levels; and avoid overly-processed vegetarian products.

Watch Out for Unhealthy Vegetarian Products

As we mentioned before, just because something is meat-free, it doesn't mean it's healthy. Lots of vegetarian products are basically garbage because of how many artificial ingredients are packed in. Learn to read labels and avoid processed food as much as possible. Fresh (or fresh that's been frozen) is always best, and that's especially true when it comes to vegetarianism.

How to Meal Prep On a Vegetarian Diet

When you're following a plant-based diet, you don't have to worry about cooking meat, but there is still good amount of prep work you can do on your chosen day to make the rest of the week easier. Here are four tips:

Buy lots of frozen vegetables

Vegetables will now make up a big part of your everyday meals, so you need to buy a lot. You can only buy and eat so much fresh produce before you need to freeze it, and that process can be a pain. You have to blanch most vegetables before you can freeze them, or they get "off" textures and flavors. To save time and energy, buy frozen when you can. There will always be certain vegetables you can't buy frozen in the store, and they can be more expensive, but staples like broccoli, peas, and green beans are usually plentiful and cheap.

Prep big portions of rice, beans, etc.

Rice, beans, lentils, and other grains make up another big part of your meals and are frequently your protein source. These can take a long time to cook, so it's a good idea to make big batches in advance. Some dried foods like beans and lentils benefit from an overnight soak (it makes them easier to digest), so get those ready the night before prep day, and then cook them.

Find good packaged vegetarian brands
We talked about how a lot of packaged vegetarian foods aren't good because they're so high in processed ingredients. There are more natural and even organic brands, however, and having some pre-prepared items on hand can be really convenient. Check out brands like Amy's Kitchen, Sweet Earth, and Eden Foods. You want the best when it comes to nut milks, meat substitutes, and more.

Meal prep on a vegetarian diet will include buying lots of frozen veggies; making big batches of grains on prep day; finding organic and unprocessed vegetarian brands; and saving your fresh veggie prep for the last minute.

Save fresh veggie prep for the last minute

You can prep a lot of vegetables on prep day by roasting them, but what about the veggies you want to eat something raw in a salad? Save that prep for last minute, since vegetables stay fresh longer when they're whole and not chopped up. You can even undercook certain vegetables like dark green leafy greens and then finish when you're getting together the last parts of the meal you'll be eating.

Chapter 5: Favorite Cooking

There are several reasons why you should use meal prepping while following a ketogenic diet plan or lifestyle.

1.The keto requires your meals follow a very specific break down of the calories you consume in each meal. (i.e. 5% carbohydrates, 20% proteins and 75% fats).

2.Planning for an entire week can help alleviate the stress of preparing each meal individually.

3.It saves time, money, and energy. Although following a keto diet plan is not expensive on its face. You could find yourself spending extra time and money repeatedly making trips to the grocery store, wasting unused food or getting takeout. Meal prepping prevents these common pitfalls.

4.Meal prepping ensures that your time is not spend slaving in the kitchen, freeing you up to spend more time with the people you care about and doing the activities you enjoy.

How to Start Keto Meal Prepping Today?

The most successful meal prepping is simple. Don't over complicate your meals. Choose simple, easy to follow recipes that include whole, nutritious foods that you like.

For example, in the beginning avoid recipes which you haven't previously made. In the beginning, go for recipes which you have prepared previously and know well. Then as you become comfortable with meal prepping, get more adventurous. Go for new recipes and innovative ideas as soon as you start getting adjusted to the process. Meal prepping is a key to success when doing any keto diet. To start efficiently meal prepping on your keto plan, follow try the following simple steps:

1.Choose a Prep Day:

Start with selecting a specific day and time to prepare your meals. This is the initial step of any meal prepping. Sunday is commonly preferred for this purpose as it is the day before the dreaded Monday work week begins, but any day that works for you is a good day to start. In the beginning consider prepping your meals for 2-3 days. You can always increase your meal amounts later. Some experienced meal prepping devotees divide their meal prepping days for a week into half i.e. Sunday and Wednesday.

2.Choose Your Meals:

Which recipe to follow and the amount to be prepared is a vital question you will want to answer before starting any meal prep. You may preferably go for dinners first, or you may opt for prepping breakfasts and lunches first. Choose various recipes for different meal times.

3.Use the Proper Jars & Containers:

Before you start any of your meal prepping make sure you have the proper storage containers and jars for the food you have prepped. Food storage can determine the success and how efficient your meal prepping is. Air tight jars and containers should be the preferred containers for meal prepping. These containers help to maintain the freshness of your food. They also typically freeze well. Don't forget a good marker to label your containers properly. The following jars and containers are best suited for meal prepping:

•Stackable

•Freezer Safe

•Microwaveable

•Reusable

•Dishwasher Safe

•Freezer Safe

•BPA Free

Chapter 6: Keto Best Practices

Write a Journal

Although it's not a requirement, you may want to start writing a personal journal or diary regarding your diet. You do not have to be a professional writer to do

this.

However, there are two things that you have to do:

• Update your journal regularly (preferably daily)

• Be completely honest with everything that you write in your journal

If you are not that fond of the actual act of writing, then you might want to use a computer or even your mobile phone. Just create a file that you can update easily. The important thing is to have something that you can write on regularly so your writings will be saved and won't be lost. These days, there are many free writings apps and software that you can easily download with just a press of a button or a click of a mouse. Of course, it is still recommended that you do it the old-fashioned way: with a notebook and a pen.

Having a journal will allow you to view yourself from a different standpoint, from a perspective that is free from any bias. This is also a good way to see how you can better improve yourself. This is why you have to update your journal regularly and be honest with every record that you write. Your journal will serve as a mirror of yourself.

Since it is your own personal journal, you are free to write everything that you want. Ideally, it should include your reasons for going on a keto diet, your objectives, your thoughts and feelings, your experiences as you go through the diet, and others. In the first few weeks, you might not fully appreciate the value of the journal, but just be more patient. After some time, you will start to appreciate just how helpful it is to have a journal, especially once you notice your progress on the diet.

Take It Easy

Do not be hard on yourself. After all, the keto diet is not meant to be a short-time diet. In fact, the idea is to make it a way of life. But, of course, you are free to use it only for a short period. The diet already has its own challenges, so you do not have to put more pressure on yourself. Take it easy and relax from time to time, especially when you feel like giving up. If you find it hard to cut down your caloric and/or carb intake at once, then aim for gradual improvements. However, do not confuse this with being lazy. Taking it easy only means that you should not stress yourself unnecessarily. It is still important that you do your best and to be serious about your diet.

Learn from Your Mistakes

Always learn from your mistakes. It is a fact that many people who go on a diet fail to stick to their diet for a variety of reasons. No matter what your reason might be for failing to stick to your diet, always learn from your mistakes. Also, instead of being too hard on yourself, make it a process of learning. You do not need to hit ketosis the first time you try to be on a keto diet. The important thing is that you do your best to be able to reach it.

After all, you can benefit from the keto diet even if you do not reach the state of ketosis, it is only when you reach a state of ketosis can you enjoy the full benefits that the keto diet offers.

The keto diet is normally a long-term diet, so there is good chance that you will commit some mistakes, such as suddenly eating lots of carbs in a day, and others. Also, if it is your first time to go on a keto diet, then you might find it very challenging and you won't stick to the idea. Another common mistake is reaching the state of ketosis but then failing to maintain it. If you ever commit any of these mistakes for whatever reason (as well as other mistakes that you might also commit), do not be too hard on yourself.

However, be sure to take some time to think about what happened, and then learn from the experience. Of course, you should also remember any new lessons that you can learn and put them into practice. When you commit a mistake, do not be discouraged. Remember that you can always try again and do better.

Develop Your Understanding

It can be hard to stick to a diet plan if you do not understand what is happening. So, it is encouraged that you read as much as you can to learn more about the keto diet. By now, you should already have a good understanding of what the keto diet is all about. Just make sure that you do not forget what you already know about the ketogenic diet.

Developing your understanding is not just limited to the keto diet itself. It also includes your understanding of yourself. Going on a keto diet is a journey that, if taken seriously can lead to self-realization. When you go keto, you will get to know more about yourself, such as your strengths and weaknesses. This is one of the best things about the diet. You do not just learn how to burn fats and be healthier, you also get to be more in touch with yourself.

Continuous Practice

Mastery of the keto diet takes lots of practice. You have to adjust and improve yourself little by little. Indeed, the keto diet is not an easy diet that will only require a few days of your time. Rather, it is about changing your lifestyle and making you healthier. As you may already know, making changes especially if you are used to an unhealthy diet is not easy to do. So, you have to keep on practicing until you get everything right. Soon enough, you will be so used to the keto diet that you would not have to spend any extraordinary effort just to stick to it. When you reach this point, then being in a state of ketosis will be your natural state. Just imagine the positive impact that this can have on your life. So, how are you supposed to stick to this diet? Well, it is as simple as always following the diet. If ever you commit a mistake and fail along the way, then be sure to bounce back as soon as possible. Keep in mind that a keto diet is a lifestyle. If you want to learn this lifestyle, then you have to live it. It is okay to commit mistakes as long as you are doing your best, and as long as you learn from every mistake.

Starting A Ketogenic Diet

Starting out on any new diet can be hard, but a ketogenic diet can be one of the hardest to start. This is because it is a sudden change to a completely different way of eating. Carbs are everywhere and we are programmed to eat as many as we can, so most of us have not had a car-free day in our entire lives. For this reason, regardless of whether we are starting by reducing our carbs, or going cold turkey, the first few days need to be as easy as possible.

Make sure that you have got rid of all your high carb foods. Some people may do this by eating them all over a week leading up to the first day. Others may throw or give the food away to remove temptation. Either way, you need it gone before you start your diet, to remove all the foods that are likely to make you give up. For this reason, it is a good idea to ask other people to keep their carby foods away as well, to prepare your own meals, and to refuse invitations to eat out for a while.

Make sure you have all the foods you will want to eat at home. Check out our recipes nearer the end of the book for an idea of what you will want to have. But the priority is a lot of leafy greens, low carb root vegetables, healthy fats, and lean proteins. If you can, try making meals in advance and freezing them in individual tuppers. And make sure to get some low carb, high fat, high protein snacks, like peanut butter, beef jerky, or boiled eggs. That way you can always have something quick to eat when you need it.

When starting out on a ketogenic diet, you will want to begin with foods you already like. Liver, kale, and almond butter are wonderful additions to a ketogenic diet, but eating things you don't like is not the best way to start a long-term diet. Instead, look through the recipe lists for recipes with foods you love, so that you can truly enjoy your diet.

Next, you will want to start on a morning, when you are not going to work. Stress makes us crave carbs more, and eating carbs is what starts the hunger cycle in the first place. So if we start with an empty stomach, running on ketones from the previous night, and we are going to have a relaxed day or two, we will be able to stick it out through the first few days. This massively improves our chances of success, as the first days are the hardest.

When you start a ketogenic diet, you will find many side effects. Most of them are harmless and just part of your body recovering from a lifetime on a high carb diet. Carb cravings are the most common symptom. We have already discussed why these happen, so it is important to remain calm and try and push through. In the next chapter we will offer some solutions for these hunger pangs, but remember that they are at their worst for only a few days, and after that they will be gone.

Indigestion can occur when you first start a ketogenic diet. This is due to a common mistake people make, assuming that this diet is low in all plants. That is not true. On this diet you will eat large amounts of high fibre, low carb plant foods, fatty fruits like avocado, and nuts and seeds. If you do not eat enough fiber you will find that your meals cause reflux, indigestion, and gut cramping. If you are eating plenty of plants but still suffering reflux, indigestion, and gut cramping, consider eliminating dairy from your diet. Sometimes following a ketogenic diet can make an underlying cow milk protein allergy come to the surface. You always would have had this allergy, but it would have been masked by other aspects of your diet.

Finally, if you suffer stomach cramps, diarrhea, or oily, black stools, then you are eating too much fat. How is it possible to eat too much fat on a low carb, high fat diet? The same way it is possible to pour too much water into a glass. When we are following a ketogenic diet we are using fat as fuel. But we can only absorb so much fat in one go, and burn so much fat. When we eat more fat than we can absorb, our bodies just let it pass through us. This is largely harmless, but has the side effect of damaging our gut bacteria, one of the exact things we are trying to fix without diet. So if you notice these side effects, start reducing your fat intake until your stools return to normal.

Besides these symptoms, you should also experience a whole host of beneficial symptoms. Some of the most beneficial symptoms, like an improvement in metabolism, and weight loss, will take longer to happen. But others happen within days. You will find your appetite begins to come under your control. As your insulin spikes and crashes disappear, your body gets used to having a steady supply of energy. This means that rather than feeling hungry every single time your blood sugar drops, and snacking between meals, you are eating a healthy meal and going straight through to the next one without feeling hungry.

You will find that yeast infections and skin conditions improve, or even disappear entirely. This is because your candida is not being fed, so it has nothing to grow from. Candida causes many types of yeast infection, and several types of skin problem, being the root cause of most cases of dandruff, for starters. It also makes other conditions, like eczema, worse, by irritating the skin and growing under and around dead skin cells.

You will find your moods are more even. That "hungry" feeling you get when your blood sugar drops is not normal. It is your body responding to a lack of glucose, trying to get you to eat carbs. At first you may feel the carb-hungry anger more intensely than usual, but after a couple of days your body gets used to not having those constant spikes and crashes in blood sugar. No energy crashes means no cravings, means no eating carbs, means no spikes, means no more crashes. It is vitally important to fight this cycle and restore order, even if you have no intention of following a ketogenic diet for life.

Chapter 6: Low-Carb

The low-carbohydrate diet has been around since the beginning of human history. Pre-agricultural humans subsisted on what they could hunt or gather, which meant wild meat, game, fish, roots, berries, and other plant matter. Around 12,000 years ago, humans left their nomadic ways and began consuming more carbohydrates in the forms of cereal grains and legumes. Still, it was a far cry from today's endless supply of pasta and breadsticks.

Fast forward to the twentieth century when industrial food products, refined grains, and sugar became widely available and came with a side of obesity, heart disease, and diabetes. Instead of blaming refined carbs—which were novel foods in human evolution—people pointed the finger at fat.

Give Up Carbs, Not Flavor

To understand why a diet low in carbohydrates is so effective, it helps to have a basic scientific understanding of how and why our bodies use and store carbohydrates.

Whenever we eat foods containing carbohydrates, our blood sugar (also known as blood glucose) levels rise proportionate to the total amount of carbohydrates we have eaten (called the glycemic load) and how quickly that carbohydrate is absorbed (called the glycemic index). The pancreas, which is an organ that's located deep in the abdomen, releases the hormone insulin, which lowers blood glucose and makes it available to the cells.

When the body doesn't need glucose for immediate energy or to restore the energy stored in the muscles (called glycogen), the glucose is repackaged with fatty acids into more complex structures called triglycerides for long-term storage within the fat cells. If there isn't enough room in the existing fat cells, new fat cells are created, aided by insulin. Insulin also activates enzymes that increase fat storage and prevent fat from being used for fuel. Hence, when blood glucose levels and insulin production remain consistently high, fat storage is inevitable and fat metabolism (that is, the use of fat for fuel) cannot occur.

A low-carbohydrate, high-fat ketogenic diet keeps insulin levels low, which allows triglycerides to be broken down into fatty acids that can be burned as energy. Not only does this result in the loss of body fat, but it also ensures that a steady stream of energy is available to fuel your body. And it tastes pretty good, too!

Have You Met These Healthy Fats?

The ketogenic diet is necessarily high in fats. But not all fats are created equal. Partially hydrogenated oils contain trans fats (even when the package says "0 grams trans-fat") and are found in margarine, peanut butter, and other processed foods. They are dangerous to your health because they increase inflammation and elevate LDL ("bad" cholesterol) and reduce HDL ("good" cholesterol), both of which increase the risk of heart disease and hinder weight loss. So just go with the real stuff. Here are my top five fats for a low-carb diet:

Avocados

Avocados are rich in monounsaturated fats, particularly oleic acid, which has been shown to decrease inflammation, lower the risk of heart disease, and improve insulin sensitivity. Monounsaturated fats are burned at a faster rate than other fats and increase metabolism. For example, a study published in 2013 found that the addition of half of an avocado with meals increased satiety for up to five hours following a meal among obese individuals. Avocados are also a great source of vitamin K, folate, vitamin C, potassium, and vitamin E. Potassium is especially important on a low-carb diet because it helps prevent muscle cramping, which can be a concern as you shed excess water weight.

Butter

It is no surprise that butter contributes flavor and a rich, velvety texture to foods, but you may be surprised to learn that butter, especially when it is sourced from organic, grass-fed cows, contains omega-3 fats, selenium, and vitamins A, D, E, and K. Butter has a low smoke point, so rather than using it for high-temperature cooking, use butter on cooked vegetables, in baking, or in quick, low-heat cooking methods, such as when making eggs. If you are sensitive to dairy proteins, try ghee (also called clarified butter), which has been heated and strained to remove the milk solids.

Coconut Oil

Coconut oil is the ketogenic dieter's best friend. It is a flavorful source of fatty acids that have been shown to correlate with increased calorie burning and weight loss. It is also easily converted into water-soluble molecules called ketone bodies in the liver, meaning you can get into ketosis more quickly by adding coconut oil to your diet (see "What Is Ketosis?" here). Coconut oil also increases metabolism while reducing appetite, so the calories you consume from coconut oil will be burned off and cause you to eat fewer other foods. It can be eaten raw in fat bombs (sweet or savory snack bites that provide nearly all of their calories from fat) or used for roasting, sautéing, or frying.

Extra-Virgin Olive Oil
Extra-virgin olive oil is rich in monounsaturated fats, contains antioxidants, is anti-inflammatory, may reduce the risk of heart disease, and ultimately can help you lose weight. For example, a study comparing the effects of a low-fat diet versus a diet enriched with extra-virgin olive oil found that women following a 1,500-calorie-a-day diet containing three tablespoons of olive oil lost twice as much weight as those consuming the same number of calories without the olive oil. For the greatest health benefits, use extra-virgin olive oil for low-heat cooking, in salad dressings, and to drizzle over cooked foods.

Nuts
Nuts such as walnuts, cashews, pistachios, almonds, and pecans contain monounsaturated and polyunsaturated fats, including omega-3 fatty acids, and can help reduce the risk of heart disease, lower diabetes risk, and encourage you to stick with your low-carb diet by improving satiety and ultimately helping you lose weight. Nuts contain about equal proportions of protein and carbohydrate, which is mostly in the form of fiber.

What Is Ketosis?

"Fat adaptation" is another term that describes ketosis. Being in ketosis naturally reduces your appetite. In fact, appetite reduction is one of the many appeals of fat adaptation because you can go for long stretches between meals—such as a busy day or a deliberate period of fasting— without feeling hungry or experiencing symptoms of low blood sugar.

In healthy people, nutritional ketosis is usually achieved within as few as three days of reducing daily carbohydrate intake to below 50 grams. However, people who are obese may have more difficulty achieving ketosis. Ketosis can also be induced by fasting, which counterintuitively may be easier for some people than eating a low-carb diet during the transition period. Always consult your physician before making any dietary changes.

A ketogenic diet may improve metabolic syndrome, insulin resistance, and type 2 diabetes. It is also used to treat people with epilepsy and other neurological disorders.

Going Keto

A ketogenic diet contains low carbohydrates, moderate protein, and high fat. The macronutrient composition of a ketogenic diet typically falls within the following ranges: 5 to 10 percent carbohydrates, 20 to 25 percent protein, and 70 percent fat. On a 2,000-calorie-per-day diet, that would look like 50 grams of carbohydrates, 100 grams of protein, and 155 grams of fat.

Some low-carbohydrate diets include very high levels of protein—as high as 50 percent of total calories. While protein promotes satiety, improves mood, and builds muscle, obtaining more than 30 percent of your calories from protein can have detrimental and even dangerous effects. Excess protein can be converted to glucose, which elevates insulin levels, hinders ketosis, and may stall weight loss. Worse yet, excess protein can cause kidney damage, weaken bones, and contribute to the growth of cancer cells.

Instead of replacing calories from carbohydrates with calories from protein, the ketogenic approach involves replacing those calories with calories from fat. Pairing a low-carbohydrate diet with a high-fat diet is essential to success because even during weight loss, your body can only burn a limited amount of stored body fat—about 69 calories per kilogram of nonessential body fat per day. You have to eat something to fuel your daily activity, and dietary fat is the best replacement for carbs. Dietary fat slows the release of glucose into the bloodstream and is satiating, so you won't feel hungry on a low-carb diet. Of course, always speak to your doctor before beginning any diet, especially if you have an existing medical condition.

Should You Count Calories?

While calories do matter even on a ketogenic diet, they don't necessarily need to be counted because ketosis results in a natural appetite reduction and reduced calorie intake. Nevertheless, calculating your basal metabolic rate (BMR) and total daily energy expenditure (TDEE) is useful for planning purposes and can be essential if you find that your weight loss has stalled on a low-carb diet.

Start Fresh

Changing your diet is challenging enough, but keeping forbidden foods around the house is a recipe for frustration. Instead, purge the carb-laden foods from your refrigerator and pantry before you begin a ketogenic diet. Here are some of the most obvious offenders:

- Bread
- Cakes
- Chips
- Cookies
- Crackers
- Cupcakes
- Legumes
- Pasta
- Potatoes
- Rice
- Snack cakes
- Sweetened beverages
- Sweetened condiments and dressings
- Syrup and other sweeteners, including honey

Stock Your Refrigerator and Pantry

Clearing forbidden foods from your pantry will make it easier to stick to the plan, and you'll have that much more room for the tasty, low-carb foods you will soon be enjoying. here are some of the most common ingredients found in the recipes in this book:

- Bacon
- Black pepper
- Butter

- Cheese (such as cheddar, Parmesan, and mozzarella)
- Coconut oil
- Cumin
- Eggs
- Extra-virgin olive oil
- Garlic
- Ginger
- Greek yogurt, whole-milk plain

- Herbs, fresh (such as basil, cilantro, and parsley)
- Nuts
- Onions
- Paprika, smoked
- Sea salt
- Stevia, liquid
- Vinegar

Your Go-To Foods

Keeping the list of common ingredients in mind, let's now take a look at why certain staples of a low-carb diet are so essential:

LEAFY GREENS provide fiber, vitamins, minerals, antioxidants, and other micronutrients. They add volume to a low-carb diet and are both beautiful and delicious. Options include kale, chard, collard greens, arugula, romaine lettuce, and spinach, among a myriad of other delicious options.

COLORFUL non-starchy vegetables are also a pretty and tasty source of fiber and micronutrients. Options are almost endless and include asparagus, broccoli, cauliflower, endive, fennel, mushrooms, onion, peppers, radishes, and spinach. Avocado, tomato, and zucchini also fall into this category though they are technically fruits.

EGGS are one of the easiest ketogenic breakfast options. When cooked with butter, they hit the exact keto ratio of 70 percent or more fat and contain no carbs. Ideally choose free-range, organic eggs for the best nutrition and environmental sustainability.

COCONUT OIL can help suppress appetite and increase your metabolism. Choose extra-virgin, cold-pressed coconut oil for the best nutrition. If you don't like the coconut flavor, choose a filtered coconut oil. Add coconut oil into your diet slowly to avoid digestive discomfort.

CHICKEN THIGHS have so much more flavor than chicken breasts and withstand longer cooking times, especially if they are bone-in. Choose free-range, organic chicken if possible and opt for skin-on, bone-in meat. Even better, purchase a whole chicken and use the bones to make Chicken Bone Broth.

BEEF is off-limits in many modern diets, but it's a staple in most ketogenic diets. The most common cuts in low-carb diets include short ribs, ground beef, and rib eye steak. Choose grass-fed beef for the best nutrition.

BACON needs no explanation, but just in case you need convincing, bacon adds flavor, fat, and a moderate amount of protein. Choose a nitrite-free, uncured bacon for the best nutrition. My favorite is Applewood smoked bacon.

FATTY FISH such as salmon, tuna, and mackerel are rich in omega-3 fatty acids and are considered heart-healthy choices. Choose wild fish whenever possible and explore sustainable options through Monterey Bay Aquarium's Seafood Watch program (SeafoodWatch.org).

BUTTER is a staple of low-carb diets, but not in the quantities you might imagine. A little goes a long way toward shifting the calorie balance to fat instead of carbs. It is especially helpful to ensure you get enough calories without overdoing it on protein. Choose butter from grass-fed cows if possible.

NUTS make great snacks and are rich in fiber and micronutrients. They also provide the crunch factor that's often lacking in low-carb diets. Choose whole nuts and weigh or measure them to ensure you're getting a proper portion. The best options are Brazil nuts, cashews, macadamia nuts, pecans, pine nuts, pistachios, and walnuts.

NO ARTIFICIAL SWEETENERS

Artificial sweeteners such as aspartame and saccharin are positively correlated with metabolic syndrome, weight gain, headaches, and even cancer. Part of the reason for their effects on weight is that they stimulate insulin production in much the same way that sugar does. Also, they train your taste buds to prefer sweet foods. Sugar alcohols are similarly problematic and often result in severe gastrointestinal distress due to their inability to be absorbed by the body.

Stevia, on the other hand, is a natural sweetener that contributes no calories or carbohydrates. However, many people with certain pollen allergies may be sensitive to stevia, so use caution when trying it for the first time. I use it sparingly in cooking, particularly for making low-carb desserts. I also use the sweetener Swerve in some baked goods. It can be used cup-for-cup to replace sugar in most recipes. It is made from erythritol, a sugar alcohol that is easier to digest than most, and which has no bitter aftertaste.

How to Reduce Carbs and Increase Flavor

You never really realize how many carbs some of your favorite foods contain until you turn over the package and start reading the nutrition label. You already know to avoid bread, potatoes, rice, and sweets on a low-carb diet, but carbs are also lurking in

unlikely places. Here are some foods to limit or avoid on a low-carb diet:
5 Surprising Sources of Carbs

CONDIMENTS:
Barbecue sauce and ketchup are filled with so much sugar that you might not be able to distinguish their nutrition facts from those of cake frosting, packing in 5 to 7 grams of sugar per tablespoon! Most prepared salad dressings contain added sugar, especially if they're reduced fat. Instead, create your own sauces and salad dressings using oil, vinegar, vegetables, herbs, and spices, as described in some of the recipes that follow.

DAIRY:
One cup of milk contains 12 grams of carbohydrates, as many as a slice of wheat bread. Yogurt can be even worse, with as many as 19 grams of carbohydrates in a cup of plain yogurt and more than twice that in the sweetened varieties. Whole-milk (or full-fat) Greek yogurt is a better option, with 9 grams of carbs per cup. Cheese and butter are the lowest- carb dairy options, with 2 grams or fewer per cup.

PEANUT BUTTER AND NUT BUTTER:
Just two tablespoons (about one ounce) of peanut butter or almond butter contain 7 grams of carbohydrates. If you're scooping it into smoothies or slathering it on low-carb bread, beware—the carbs and calories add up quickly! Only use the amounts specified in the recipes. Otherwise, whole nuts are a better option. Macadamia nuts, walnuts, and pecans all have fewer than 4 grams of carbs per ounce.

PROTEIN BARS:

Processed protein supplements such as bars and powders can contain more than 20 grams of carbs per serving depending on the brand. Instead of these convenience foods, choose whole-food sources of protein such as fish, meat, eggs, nuts, and seeds, or select protein powder that is sweetened with stevia.

SUGAR-FREE FOODS:

Even sugar-free foods such as pudding, jams, and cookies are often still loaded with carbs. Sugar-free jam has 5 grams of carbs per tablespoon and sugar-free pudding has 12 grams per half-cup serving. That's not to mention the artificial sweeteners, preservatives, and other chemicals these foods contain.

Ready for some good news? Some of the most flavorful foods and cooking techniques add virtually no carbs and make your ketogenic meals taste really good! And it goes without saying that just adding butter makes everything taste better. Here are my top five tips for boosting flavor on a low-carb diet:

5 Tips for Adding Flavor

ADD VINEGAR:

Vinegars such as balsamic, red wine, white wine, and sherry all brighten the flavors of virtually any dish without adding carbs. I like to add a splash of vinegar near the end of the cooking period and adjust to taste. Cooking with a splash of red or white wine also boosts flavor. The alcohol cooks off in just a few minutes, leaving no carbs and a complex flavor.

COOK WITH BROTH:

Use Chicken Bone Broth (here) or Beef Bone Broth (here) to braise meat, cook vegetables, stir into sauces, and of course as a base for soup.

ROAST VEGETABLES:
 Steaming vegetables preserves more nutrients, but roasted vegetables have an unbeatable flavor. Cook them with a generous amount of fat on a baking sheet in a hot oven for the best results.

SEAR MEAT:
 Cook meat briefly over high heat with a bit of fat to produce a golden-brown crust. Do this for quick-cooking steaks and chicken or tougher cuts of meat before adding wine or broth for a long, slow simmer.

USE FRESH HERBS:
 While dried herbs boast a long shelf life, they don't compare to fresh when it comes to flavor. Woody herbs such as thyme and rosemary can withstand long cooking periods. More delicate herbs such as cilantro, dill, and basil should be added near the end of the cooking time to get the most flavor.

Tips And Tricks For Handling Carb Cravings

Carb cravings are one of the hardest parts of cutting your carb intake right back. We have already discussed why our bodies resist going low carb so aggressively, but that is of little comfort to someone who is going through the cravings themselves. Instead, here are some helpful ways of coping with the carb cravings until they naturally pass.

1: Sweeteners

Although artificial sweeteners are hardly a health tonic, they can make for a very useful tool when controlling our carb cravings. Consider natural forms of sweeteners first, but most of them have a small amount of carbs, so if you will be using a lot, choose artificial ones.

Some people advise against using sweeteners, claiming that they will prolong the psychological addiction to carbs. However, although this is slightly true, it isn't the point. The physical addiction to carbs is far more intense than any psychological addiction, and if we go long enough without too many carbs, that addiction will break. After we have defeated the physical aspect of our addiction we can then consider cutting out sweeteners and fighting the psychological aspect. But until then, sweeteners are very useful.

2: Eat more protein

Sometimes when we crave carbs we are just plain hungry. After so long eating too many carbs, all day every day, with every meal, our stomach rumbles and carbs are the first thing we try to get to eat. This means that we need to retrain our appetite signals to crave different foods, not just sugars and starches. And the first step to that is eating more protein. Eating protein fills our stomachs and triggers the release of hormones that make us feel satisfied. So if we need calories, protein should help.

3: Fill up on greens

The annoying part of carb cravings, though, is that because they are so misdirected, they could be a craving for any vital nutrient. If eating protein doesn't satisfy you, then it might be that you need vitamins and minerals. A large green salad, or a low carb stir-fry or soup, will fill your stomach with fiber, and add vital nutrients to your diet. This can take longer to have an effect, so be patient. If it works and you feel better, increase your daily greens intake until you no longer feel cravings.

4: Drink some water

And if protein and greens both fail, you might actually just be thirsty. This is an incredibly common problem for people who do not drink many fluids, or for people who only drink sweetened beverages. When you rarely drink clean, simple water, your body doesn't know how to ask for it. Instead, it will fire up your appetite signals as soon as you get dehydrated. Get a glass of water and drink it quickly. Then get a second glass and sip it over half an hour. This rehydration might make your cravings go away.

5: Go for a walk

Finally, if nothing hits the spot for your cravings, try and distract yourself. Mental activity can be hard in the middle of carb cravings, and idle distractions like watching television don't really take anything away from it. Instead, try and get moving. A walk around the block, or through some fields, can really take your mind away from cravings. And exercise, at least whilst you're doing it, will help you fight hunger. Just make sure to have a healthy meal ready for when you are done exercising.

6: Meditate

Mindfulness is a great way of fighting cravings. You know, on a conscious level, that your cravings for carbs are not a vital need, that your body is misleading you, and that the cravings will go away. But your body, your primitive self, does not know that. It is thought that meditation is a way of communicating with your body and cooperating with each other. Some Buddhist monks can sit on solid ice blocks bare naked, or even slow their heart rates right down, without suffering harm, just by meditating and focusing on their bodies. Even if you have never meditated a day in your life, you may find it beneficial to give it a go.

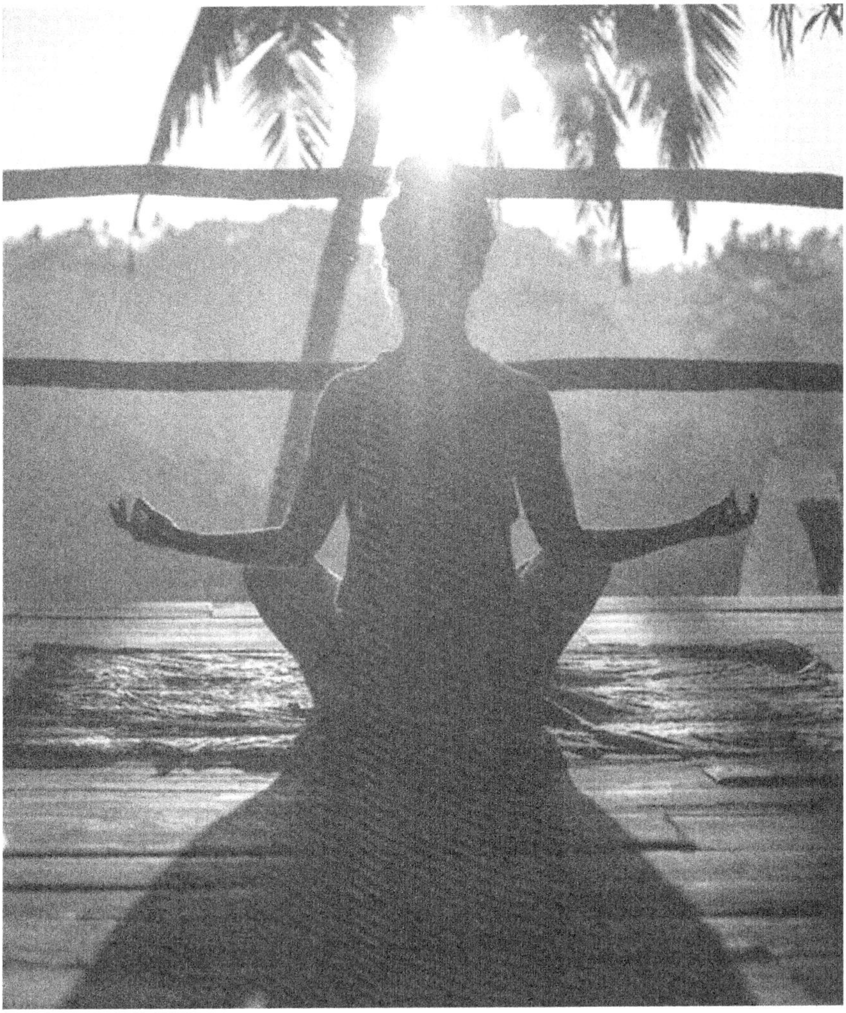

Chapter 8: Ingredients for Meal Prepping

Kitchen Equipment

To be ready for meal prepping, you need to be armed with the right supplies. Start with the "must-have" list and move on to the "nice-to-have" supplies once you get started. It won't take long to figure out what works best for you.

Must-Have Supplies

Baking sheet: From roasting vegetables to toasting granola to baking whole-grain pizza, baking sheets will serve as an all-purpose cooking vessel in your kitchen. They're lightweight, inexpensive, and durable. Make sure your kitchen is stocked with at least two.

Cast iron pan: Although it takes a bit longer to heat, a cast iron pan is very versatile and can be used to cook an array of dishes like steak and grain-based dishes. It's great to use on the stove and in the oven. Cast iron is reliable, long-lasting, ruggedly handsome, and easy to maintain.

Sauté pan: A 12-inch, straight-sided sauté pan has a larger bottom surface area and better protects against splattering. There's also lots of room for making double batches, and it can easily be transferred to the oven.

Muffin tins: Muffin tins aren't just for muffins. I like to use them to cook other dishes like mini quiches and meatballs. I recommend getting one regular and one mini tray. It's always nice to mix and match the sizes for meals and snacks.

Blender: You don't need to invest hundreds of dollars in a fancy blender. You'll get a lot of use out of your blender when making smoothies, sauces, and dips (like hummus). When cleaning your blender, make sure to take it apart entirely so you can clean the blender blades properly.

Measuring cups and spoons: Portion control is essential when eating healthy. If you over pour oil, for example, it can add hundreds of unnecessary calories to a recipe, as 1 tablespoon of any oil contains 120 calories. The same goes for baked goods—if a recipe calls for ¼ cup of chopped nuts, measure it out so you don't end up adding hundreds of extra calories to the dish.

NICE-TO-HAVE SUPPLIES

Slow cooker: A slow cooker will change your life! Purchase a larger-size one (8-quart, or bigger) that can be used for double (or even triple) batches of chili, soup, and chicken or beef dishes, which can be frozen for later. I recently purchased an inexpensive slow cooker (no bells or whistles on this one) and can't believe how little work is involved to make a tasty meal.

Mixing bowls: Many recipes call for mixing batters or ingredients. I recommend a set of mixing bowls that have nonslip bottoms, solid construction, and nontoxic lids. Dishwasher- and freezer-safe is a plus. Although many mixing bowl sets can be expensive, shop around and you can find a good set for a good price.

Good utensils: If your cooking utensils need an update, once you get into the swing of things with meal prepping, you'll want to update these kitchen tool essentials. Purchase a spatula, a few wooden spoons (they're usually sold in packs), and a ladle. If you have a nonstick pan, opt for a plastic or silicon-coated spatula to avoid damaging the pan's surface.

Cutting board: Plastic cutting boards are inexpensive and are dishwasher-safe. Bamboo and wooden cutting boards must be washed by hand and tend to warp a little quicker. If any cutting board ends up with nicks and grooves from lots of use, it should be replaced immediately. The grooves can harbor microorganisms, which can end up in your food.

Good set of knives: You don't need to spend hundreds of dollars on a new set of knives, but a good chef's knife and paring knife can make meal prepping go that much more smoothly. The chef's knife is perfect for slicing meat, cutting vegetables, and chopping herbs and nuts. A paring knife is perfect for smaller tasks like peeling potatoes, seeding peppers, or segmenting orange slices.

Chapter 9: Meal Prep Recipes

Breakfast

Scrambled Eggs

(Total Time: 10 Min|Serves: 1)

Ingredients:

- 4 bell mushrooms, chopped
- 3 eggs, whisked
- Salt and ground black pepper, to taste
- 2 ham slices, chopped
- ¼ cup red bell pepper, seeded and chopped
- ½ cup spinach, chopped
- 1 tablespoon coconut oil

Directions:

Heat up a pan with half of the oil over medium heat, add the mushrooms, spinach, ham, and bell pepper, stir, and cook for 4 minutes. Heat up another pan with the rest of the oil over medium heat, add the eggs, and scramble them. Add the vegetables, ham, salt, and pepper stir, cook for 1 minute, and serve.

Breakfast Casserole

(Total Time: 40 Min|Serves: 4)

Ingredients:

- 10 eggs
- 1 pound pork sausage, chopped
- 1 onion, peeled and chopped
- 3 cups spinach, torn
- Salt and ground black pepper, to taste
- 3 tablespoons avocado oil

Directions:

1 tablespoon oil should be heat up a pan over medium heat, add the sausage, stir, and brown it for 4 minutes.

Add the onion, stir, and cook for 3 minutes. Add the spinach, stir, and cook for 1 minute. Grease a baking dish with the rest of the oil, and spread the sausage mixture in it. Whisk the eggs, and add them to sausage mixture. Stir gently, place in an oven at 350°F, and bake for 30 minutes. Before serving, let the casserole cool.

Vegetable Breakfast Bread

(Total Time: 25 Min|Serves: 7)

Ingredients:

- 1 cauliflower head, separated into florets

- ½ cup fresh parsley, chopped
- 1 cup spinach, torn
- 1 onion, peeled and chopped
- 1 tablespoon coconut oil
- ½ cup pecans, ground
- 3 eggs
- 2 garlic cloves, peeled and minced
- Salt and ground black pepper, to taste

Directions:

In a food processor, mix the cauliflower florets with some salt, and pepper, and pulse well. Heat up a pan with the oil over medium heat, add the cauliflower, onion, and garlic, some salt and pepper, stir, and cook for 10 minutes. In a bowl, mix the eggs with salt, pepper, parsley, spinach, and nuts, and stir. Add the cauliflower mixture, and stir well. Spread this mixture into forms placed on a baking sheet, heat oven to 350°F, and bake for 15 minutes. Serve warm.

Breakfast Muffins

(Total Time: 30 Min|Serves: 4)

Ingredients:

- ½ cup almond milk

- 6 eggs
- 1 tablespoon coconut oil
- Salt and ground black pepper, to taste
- ¼ cup kale, chopped
- 8 prosciutto slices
- ¼ cup fresh chives, chopped

Directions:

In a bowl, mix the eggs with salt, pepper, milk, chives, and kale. Grease a muffin tray with melted coconut oil, line with prosciutto slices, pour the eggs mixture, place in an oven, and bake at 350°F for 30 minutes. Transfer muffins to a platter, and serve.

Eggs Baked in Avocados

(Total Time: 20 Min|Serves: 4

Ingredients:

- 2 avocados, cut in half and pitted
- 4 eggs
- Salt and ground black pepper, to taste
- 1 tablespoon fresh chives, chopped

Directions:

Scoop some flesh from the avocado halves, and arrange them in a baking dish. Crack an egg in each avocado, season with salt, and pepper, introduce them in the oven at 425°F, and bake for 20 minutes. Sprinkle chives at the end and serve.

Chicken Breakfast Muffins

(Total Time: 30 Min|Serves: 4)

Ingredients:

- ¾ pound chicken breast, boneless
- Salt and ground black pepper, to taste
- ½ teaspoon garlic powder
- 3 tablespoons hot sauce mixed with 3 tablespoons melted coconut oil
- 6 eggs
- 2 tablespoons green onions, chopped

Directions:

Season the chicken breast with salt, pepper, and garlic powder, place it on a lined baking sheet and bake in the oven at 425°F for 25 minutes. Transfer the chicken breast to a bowl, shred with a fork, and mix with half of the hot sauce and melted coconut oil. Toss to coat, and set aside. In a bowl, mix the eggs with salt, pepper, green onions, and the rest of the hot sauce mixed with oil and whisk. Divide this mixture into a muffin tray, top each with shredded chicken, place in an oven at 350°F, and bake for 30 minutes. Serve the muffins hot.

Breakfast Pie

(Total Time: 45 Min|Serves: 8)

Ingredients:

- ½ onion, peeled and chopped
- 1 pie crust
- ½ red bell pepper, seeded and chopped
- ¾ pound ground beef
- Salt and ground black pepper, to taste
- 3 tablespoons taco seasoning
- ½ cup fresh cilantro, chopped
- 8 eggs
- 1 teaspoon coconut oil
- 1 teaspoon baking soda
- Mango salsa, for serving

Directions:

Heat up a pan with the oil over medium heat, add the beef, cook until it browns, and mix with salt, pepper, and taco seasoning. Stir again, transfer to a bowl, and set aside. Heat up the pan again over medium heat with cooking juices from the meat, add the onion and bell pepper, stir, and cook for 4 minutes. Add the eggs, baking soda, and some salt, and stir well. Add the cilantro, stir again, and take off the heat. Spread the beef mixture in pie crust, add the vegetable mixture, and spread over meat, place in an oven at 350°F, and bake for 45 minutes. Let the pie cool, slice, divide between plates and serve with mango salsa on top.

Breakfast Stir-fry

(Total Time: 30 Min|Serves: 2)

Ingredients:

- ½ pounds minced beef
- 2 teaspoons red chili flakes
- 1 tablespoon tamari sauce
- 2 bell peppers, seeded and chopped
- 1 teaspoon chili powder
- 1 tablespoon coconut oil
- Salt and ground black pepper, to taste

For the bok choy:

- 6 bunches bok choy, trimmed and chopped
- 1 teaspoon fresh ginger, grated
- Salt, to taste
- 1 tablespoon coconut oil

For the eggs:

- 1 tablespoon coconut oil
- 2 eggs

Directions:

Heat up a pan with 1 tablespoon coconut oil over medium-high heat, add the beef and bell peppers, stir, and cook for 10 minutes. Add the salt, pepper, tamari sauce, chili flakes, and chili powder, stir, cook for 4 minutes, and take off the heat. Heat up another pan with 1 tablespoon oil over medium heat, add the bok choy, stir, and cook for 3 minutes. Add the salt, and ginger, stir, cook for 2 minutes, and take off the heat. Heat up the third pan with 1 tablespoon oil over medium heat, crack the eggs, and fry them. Divide the beef and bell pepper mixture into 2 bowls. Divide the bok choy and top with the eggs.

Breakfast Skillet

(Total Time: 30 Min|Serves: 4)

Ingredients:

- 8 ounces mushrooms, chopped

- Salt and ground black pepper, to taste
- 1 pound minced pork
- 1 tablespoon coconut oil
- ½ teaspoon garlic powder
- ½ teaspoon dried basil
- 2 tablespoons Dijon mustard
- 2 zucchini, chopped

Directions:

Heat up a pan with the oil over medium-high heat, add the mushrooms, stir, and cook for 4 minutes. Add the zucchini, salt, and pepper, stir, and cook for 4 minutes. Add the pork, garlic powder, basil, and more salt and pepper, stir, and cook until meat is done. Add the mustard, stir, cook for 3 minutes, divide into bowls, and serve.

Breakfast Bowl

(Total Time: 20 Min|Serves: 1)

Ingredients:

- 4 ounces ground beef
- 1 onion, peeled and chopped
- 8 mushrooms, sliced

- Salt and ground black pepper, to taste
- 2 eggs, whisked
- 1 tablespoon coconut oil
- ½ teaspoon smoked paprika
- 1 avocado, pitted, peeled, and chopped
- 12 black olives, pitted and sliced

Directions:

Over medium heat the coconut oil in the pan, add the onions, mushrooms, salt, and pepper, stir, and cook for 5 minutes. Add the beef, and paprika, stir, cook for 10 minutes, and transfer to a bowl. Heat up the pan again over medium heat, add the eggs, some salt, and pepper, and scramble them. Return beef mixture to pan and stir. Add the avocado and olives, stir, and cook for 1 minute. Transfer to a bowl and serve.

Breadless Breakfast Sandwich

(Total Time: 10 Min|Serves: 1)

Ingredients:

- 2 eggs
- Salt and ground black pepper, to taste
- 2 tablespoons butter

- ¼ pound pork sausage, minced
- ¼ cup water
- 1 tablespoon guacamole

Directions:

In a bowl, mix the minced sausage meat with some salt and pepper, and stir well. Shape a patty from this mixture and place it on a working surface. Heat up a pan with 1 tablespoon butter over medium heat, add the sausage patty, fry for 3 minutes on each side, and transfer to a plate. Crack an egg into 2 bowls and whisk them with some salt and pepper. Heat up a pan with the rest of the butter over medium-high heat, place 2 biscuit cutters that you've greased with some butter in the pan and add an egg to each one. Add the water to the pan, reduce heat, cover pan, and cook eggs for 3 minutes. Transfer these egg "buns" to paper towels and drain the excess grease.

Place sausage patty on one egg "bun," spread guacamole over it, and top with the other egg "bun,"

Shrimp and Bacon Breakfast

(Total Time: 15 Min|Serves: 4)

Ingredients:

- 1 cup mushrooms, sliced
- 4 bacon slices, chopped

- 4 ounces smoked salmon, chopped
- 4 ounces shrimp, deveined
- Salt and ground black pepper, to taste
- ½ cup coconut cream

Directions:

Heat up a pan over medium heat, add the bacon, stir, and cook for 5 minutes. Add the mushrooms, stir, and cook for 5 minutes. Add the salmon, stir, and cook for 3 minutes. Add the shrimp, and cook for 2 minutes. Add the salt, pepper, and coconut cream, stir, cook for 1 minute, take off the heat, and divide on plates.

Feta and Asparagus Delight

(Total Time: 25 Min|Serves: 2)

Ingredients:

- 12 asparagus spears
- 1 tablespoon olive oil
- 2 green onions, chopped
- 1 garlic clove, peeled and minced
- 6 eggs
- Salt and ground black pepper, to taste
- ½ cup feta cheese

Directions:

Heat up a pan with some water over medium heat, add the asparagus, cook for 8 minutes, drain well, chop 2 spears, and reserve the rest. Heat up a pan with the oil over medium heat, add the garlic, chopped asparagus, and onions, stir, and cook for 5 minutes. Add the eggs, salt, and pepper, stir, cover, and cook for 5 minutes. Arrange the asparagus spears on top of the frittata, sprinkle cheese, place in an oven at 350°F, and bake for 9 minutes. Divide on plates and serve.

Frittata

(Total Time: 60 Min|Serves: 4)

Ingredients:

- 9 ounces spinach
- 12 eggs
- 1-ounce pepperoni
- 1 teaspoon garlic, minced
- Salt and ground black pepper, to taste
- 5 ounces mozzarella cheese, shredded
- ½ cup Parmesan cheese, grated
- ½ cup ricotta cheese
- 4 tablespoons olive oil
- A pinch of nutmeg

Directions:

Squeeze liquid from spinach and put the spinach in a bowl. In another bowl, mix the eggs with salt, pepper, nutmeg, and garlic, and whisk. Add the spinach, Parmesan cheese, and ricotta cheese, and whisk. Pour this mixture into a pan, sprinkle with mozzarella cheese and pepperoni on top, place in an oven, and bake at 375°F for 45 minutes. Let the Let the frittata cool down for a few minutes before serving.

Sausage Patties

(Total Time: 10 Min|Serves: 4)

Ingredients:

- 1 pound minced pork
- Salt and ground black pepper, to taste
- ¼ teaspoon dried thyme
- ½ teaspoon dried sage
- ¼ teaspoon ground ginger
- 3 tablespoon cold water
- 1 tablespoon coconut oil

Directions:

Put the meat in a bowl. In another bowl, mix the water with salt, pepper, sage, thyme, and ginger, and whisk.

Add this to the meat, and stir well. Shape the patties and place them on a working surface. Heat up a pan with the coconut oil over medium-high heat, add the patties, fry them for 5 minutes, flip, and cook them for 3 minutes. Serve warm.

Smoked Salmon Breakfast

(Total Time: 10 Min|Serves: 3)

Ingredients:

- 4 eggs, whisked
- ½ teaspoon avocado oil

- 4 ounces smoked salmon, chopped

For the sauce:

- 1 cup coconut milk
- ½ cup cashews, soaked and drained
- ¼ cup green onions, chopped
- 1 teaspoon garlic powder
- Salt and ground black pepper, to taste
- 1 tablespoon lemon juice

Directions:

In a blender, mix the cashews with coconut milk, garlic powder, and lemon juice and blend well. Add the salt, pepper, and green onions, blend again, transfer to a bowl, and place it in the refrigerator. Heat up a pan with the oil over medium-low heat, add the eggs, whisk, and cook until they are almost done. Divide the eggs on plates after preheating, top with smoked salmon, and serve with the green onion sauce on top.

Seasoned Hard-boiled Eggs

(Total Time: 4 Min|Serves: 12)

Ingredients:

- 4 tea bags

- 4 tablespoons salt
- 12 eggs
- 2 tablespoons ground cinnamon
- 6 star anise
- 1 teaspoon ground black pepper
- 1 tablespoons peppercorns
- 8 cups water
- 1 cup tamari sauce

Directions:

Put water in a pot, add the eggs, bring them to a boil over medium heat, and cook until they are hard boiled.

Cool them down, and crack them without peeling. In a large pot, mix water with tea bags, salt, pepper, peppercorns, cinnamon, star anise, and tamari sauce. Add the cracked eggs, cover pot, bring to a simmer over low heat, and cook for 30 minutes. Discard tea bags, and cook eggs for 3 hours and 30 minutes. Let the eggs to cool down, peel, and serve them.

Eggs and Sausages

(Total Time: 35 Min|Serves: 6)

Ingredients:

- 5 tablespoons butter
- 12 eggs
- Salt and ground black pepper, to taste
- 1-ounce spinach, torn
- 12 ham slices
- 2 sausages, chopped
- 1 onion, peeled and chopped
- 1 red bell pepper, seeded and chopped

Directions:

Heat up a pan with 1 tablespoon butter over medium heat, add the sausages and onion, stir, and cook for 5 minutes. Add the bell pepper, salt, and pepper, stir, and cook for 3 minutes, and transfer to a bowl. Melt the rest of the butter, and divide into 12 cupcake molds. Add a slice of ham to each cupcake mold, divide the spinach in each and then the sausage mixture. Crack an egg on top, place in an oven, and bake at 425 degrees Fahrenheit for 20 minutes. Let them cool briefly before serving.

Mexican Breakfast

(Total Time: 30 Min|Serves: 8)

Ingredients:

- ½ cup enchilada sauce

- 1 pound ground pork
- 1 pound chorizo, chopped
- Salt and ground black pepper, to taste
- 8 eggs
- 1 tomato, cored and chopped
- 3 tablespoons butter
- ½ cup onion, chopped
- 1 avocado, pitted, peeled, and chopped

Directions:

In a bowl, mix the pork with chorizo, stir, and spread on a lined baking sheet. Spread enchilada sauce on top, place in an oven at 350°F, and bake for 20 minutes. Heat up a pan with the butter over medium heat, add the eggs, and scramble them. Take the pork mixture out of the oven and spread the scrambled eggs over them. Sprinkle the salt, pepper, tomato, onion, and avocado on top, divide on plates and serve.

Lunch

Caesar Salad

(Total Time: 0 Min|Serves: 2)

Ingredients:

- 1 avocado, pitted, peeled, and sliced
- Salt and ground black pepper, to taste
- 3 tablespoons creamy Caesar dressing
- 1 cup bacon, cooked and crumbled
- 1 chicken breast, grilled and shredded

Directions:

In a salad bowl, mix the avocado with bacon and chicken breast, and stir. Add the dressing, salt, and pepper, toss to coat, divide into 2 bowls, and serve.

Chicken Lettuce Wraps

(Total Time: 10 Min|Serves: 1)
Calories: 145

Total Fat: 1g;

Protein: 35g;

Dietary Fiber: 1g;

Total Carbs: 4g

Sugar: 0g;

Sodium: 100mg

Ingredients:

1 chicken breast, boneless, diced into 1-inch size pieces

1 cup diced or sliced fresh mushrooms

½ cup diced water chestnuts (from a can, drained)

1 T olive oil

1 T onion, minced

1 T minced garlic

1 T teriyaki sauce

garlic powder, only a dash

onion powder, just a dash

oregano, one dash

cayenne pepper, a small dash

salt /pepper

Directions:

Mix the ingredients and cook in a skillet until the chicken is done, about 10 minutes.

Shred the chicken

Place in leaves and roll

Freezing Instructions

Place all ingredients into one freezer bag except the lettuce. Microwave one minute and serve.

Pizza Rolls

(Total Time: 30 Min|Serves: 6)

Ingredients:

- ¼ cup mixed red and green bell peppers, seeded and chopped
- 2 cup mozzarella cheese, shredded
- 1 teaspoon pizza seasoning
- 2 tablespoons onion, peeled and chopped
- 1 tomato, cored and chopped
- Salt and ground black pepper, to taste
- ¼ cup pizza sauce
- ½ cup sausage, crumbled and cooked

Directions:

Spread the mozzarella cheese on a lined and lightly greased baking sheet, sprinkle pizza seasoning on top, place in an oven at 400°F, and bake for 20 minutes. Take the pizza crust out of the oven, spread the sausage, onion, bell peppers, and tomatoes all over, and drizzle the tomato sauce on top. Place in an oven again, and bake for 10 minutes. Take pizza out of the oven, set aside for a couple of minutes, slice into 6 pieces, roll each piece, and serve.

Spinach Stuffed Portobello Mushrooms

(Total Time: 28 Min|Serves: 4)
Calories: 373

Total Fat: 28g;

Protein: 23g;

Total Carbs: 7g

Dietary Fiber: 1g;

Sugar: 2g;

Sodium: 681mg

Ingredients:

4 Portobello mushroom tops

salt /pepper amount to taste

1 cup of ricotta cheese

1 cup chopped baby spinach

½ cup Parmesan cheese, hand-shredded

1 small can chopped or sliced black olives (2.25 oz.)

½ cup chunky vegetable marinara sauce

¼ cup mozzarella cheese, finely hand-shredded

Directions:

Set the oven to 450F.

Line a 9 x 13 inch baking pan with some parchment paper.

Place the mushrooms smooth side against the parchment paper.

salt /pepper

Cook for about 24 minutes. Then remove it from heat source and pour off the liquid.

Mix the remaining ingredients except for the mozzarella cheese. Stuff into the tops of the mushrooms.

Bake 9 min.

Remove from heat source and sprinkle the top with the hand-shredded mozzarella.

Broil until the cheese is golden and melted. Serve.

Freezing Instructions

Freeze in individual zip-lock bags. Microwave for 2 minutes to serve.

Albacore Tuna Vinaigrette Salad

(Total Time: 7 Min|Serves: 4)
Calories: 231

Total Fat: 20g;

Protein: 9g;

Total Carbs: 5.5g

Dietary Fiber: 5g;

Sugar: 0g;

Sodium: 265mg

Ingredients:

1 can albacore tuna, drained

1 pound of fresh or frozen asparagus

¼ cup walnuts, chopped

4 cups baby salad mix

½ tsp salt

¼ tsp pepper

3 tsp finely chopped onion

1 tsp spicy brown mustard

2 tsp wine vinegar, white or red

¼ cup olive oil or garlic sesame oil

1 Splenda packet

Directions:

Mix together the spices and the tuna, set aside.

Steam the asparagus for 5-7 minutes until desired crispness.

Place the salad mixture onto 4 plates.

Divide the asparagus by 4 and place on salad greens.

Divide the seasoned tuna by 4 and scatter onto the asparagus and salad.

Sprinkle each salad with the walnuts and serve.

Prep Instructions:

Place the tuna mixture in a zip-lock bag and place in the fridge. Steam the asparagus and place in a zip-lock bag in the fridge. Place the salad mix in zip-locks in the fridge. Put the walnuts in a bag in the fridge.

Chicken Quesadillas

(Total Time: 4 Min|Serves: 4)
Calories: 425g

Total Fat: 25g;

Protein: 44g;

Total Carbs: 10g

Dietary Fiber: 9g;

Sugar: 2g;

Sodium: 186mg

Ingredients:

1 cup pepper jack cheese, hand-shredded

8 tortillas Tortilla Factory Low Carb Whole Wheat Tortillas

8 oz. cooked and shredded Chicken Breast

1 chopped and Roasted Bell Pepper

2 T Cilantro

2 T Butter

1 cup plain Greek yogurt

Directions:

Place ½ pat of butter in a skillet

Mix all the ingredients in a bowl except the yogurt

Place meat ingredients inside tortillas

Toast each side

Cut into 4 wedges

Top with yogurt and salsa, if desired

Freezing Instructions:

Freeze in zip-lock bags. Place the yogurt in the fridge. Heat one minute in the microwave to thaw.

Shrimp and Cucumber Salad

(Total Time: 0 Min|Serves: 4)
Calories: 26g

Total Fat: 0g;

Protein: 2g;

Total Carbs: 3g

Dietary Fiber: 2g;

Sugar: 2g;

Sodium: 157mg

Ingredients:

2 English cucumbers

1/4 cup of red wine vinegar

2 tsp of Splenda

1/4 tsp salt

½ cup cooked shrimp

Directions:

Peel the cucumbers so that they have stripes down the side.

Slice the cucumbers as thin as you can.

Mix the dressing of sugar, salt, and vinegar very well

Place the cucumbers on a plate

Place the shrimp on top

Add the dressing and serve.

Prep Directions:

Create the entire salad and place in a covered container in the fridge. Will keep 2 days.

Turkey Wraps

(Total Time: 0 Min|Serves: 1)
Calories: 154

Total Fat: 9g;

Protein: 12g;

Dietary Fiber: 0g;

Total Carbs: 2g

Sugar: 0g;

Sodium: 250mg

Ingredients:

2 slices deli turkey

1 oz. provolone cheese, sliced

1 lettuce leaf

1 tsp spicy brown mustard

Directions:

Place turkey on the lettuce leaf

Spread with brown mustard

Top with the Provolone cheese

Roll into a burrito shape

Prep Instructions:

Roll and prepare the wraps. Place on a paper towel. Place inside a zip-lock bag. Refrigerate until served.

Feta Cucumber Salad

(Total Time: 0 Min|Serves: 4)
Calories: 142

Total Fat: 10g;

Protein: 4g;

Total Carbs: 7g

Dietary Fiber: 3g;

Sugar: 0g;

Sodium: 144mg

Ingredients:

1 head of leaf lettuce, coarsely chopped

1 c baby spinach, trimmed, coarsely chopped

½ c diced red onion

1 c grape tomatoes, sliced in half

¼ c Feta cheese, crumbled

2 cups plain greek yogurt

2 T garlic powder

1 T dill

2 T lemon juice

2 English cucumbers, chopped with peels on

2 T olive oil

¼ tsp black pepper

1 small can black olives, sliced and drained (2.25 oz. can)

½ tsp mint or 3 mint leaves

Directions:

Combine Greek yogurt, dill, garlic powder, mint, lemon juice, olive oil, ½ cup diced cucumber, and black pepper and emulsify by blending.

Taste and add salt. Add water by tablespoons if too thick.

Arrange on 4 plates the lettuce and spinach, tomatoes, cucumbers, and black olives.

Pour the dressing over the salad.

Top with the feta cheese.

Prep Directions:

Mix the salad dressing and place in fridge in closed containers. Mix the salad and bag or place in covered containers in the fridge.

Place the feta cheese in a zip-lock bag in the fridge.

Cream of Mushroom Soup

(Total Time: 4 Min|Serves: 4)
Calories: 210

Total Fat: 17g;

Protein: 10g;

Total Carbs: 3g

Dietary Fiber: 0.5g;

Sugar: 0g;

Sodium: 370mg

Ingredients:

1 pound mushrooms, sliced

1 T butter

¼ cup cream

1 cup water

¼ grated Parmesan cheese

dash of basil

dash of black pepper

Directions:

Microwave the mushrooms in the water for 4 minutes. Taste for the desired doneness.

Drain the mushrooms.

Place in blender with butter and cream and Parmesan.

Blend until creamy.

Pour into bowl and serve

Freezing Instructions:

Freeze cooked soup in one cup containers. Microwave one minute, stir, and microwave one more minute to serve.

Chili Mac

(Total Time: 9 Min|Serves: 4)
Calories: 480

Total Fat: 24g;

Protein: 36g;

Total Carbs: 25g

Dietary Fiber: 6g;

Sugar: 4g;

Sodium: 995mg

Ingredients:

1 lb ground Sirloin

1 chopped Onion

1 Chili Seasoning Mix, packet

1 cup tomato sauce

1 small can of Chunky Diced Tomatoes & Green Chilies

1 cup hand-shredded sharp cheddar

1 packet Splenda

½ cup Barilla Proteinplus Elbow macaroni

Directions:

Boil Barilla Proteinplus Elbow macaroni until done, drain.

Brown the sirloin and onions in a large skillet.

Add the pasta, tomato sauce, diced tomatoes and green chilies, and chili seasoning mix.

Taste to see if you need to add water.

Serve in 4 bowls, topping each bowl with the cheddar cheese.

Freezer Directions:

Place in four containers with lids, freeze. Microwave 2 minutes to thaw.

Barbecue Chicken Pizza

(Total Time: 29 Min|Serves: 8) Calories: 285

Total Fat: 12g;

Protein: 27g

Total Carbs: 7g

Dietary Fiber: 5g;

Sugar: 0g;

Sodium: 100mg

Ingredients:

1/2 cup G Hughes Smokehouse BBQ Sauce, sugar free

½ tsp salt

2 cups baking mix, low-carb

1 cup water

1 chopped red onion

1 cup cooked chicken, diced

½ cup chopped bell peppers, red, green, yellow assortment

½ cup sliced black olives

3 T olive oil

1 cup mozzarella cheese, hand-shredded

½ c parmesan cheese, hand-shredded

1 packet Splenda or sweetener of your choice

Directions:

Set oven to 425 F.

Mix into a dough the baking powder, baking mix, Splenda, salt, water, and oil.

Place of waxed paper and lightly oil. Roll into your pizza crust.

Bake for 9 minutes.

Remove from heat source and spread the barbecue sauce onto the crust.

Layer the toppings, placing the cheeses on top.

Bake 15 more minutes until thoroughly warmed and the cheese is melted.

Slice into 8 pieces and serve.

Freezing Directions:

Place individual slices in a zip-lock freezer bag. Freeze. To serve, heat in microwave one minute.

Cobb Salad

(Total Time: 9 Min|Serves: 1)
Calories: 561

Total Fat: 34g;

Protein: 51g;

Total Carbs: 3.9g

Dietary Fiber: 6g;

Sugar: 1g;

Sodium: 802mg

Ingredients:

1 slice Bacon or 1 T real bacon bits

1 grilled Chicken Breast, which has been cut into thin strips

1 cup Spring Mix Salad

1/2 cup grape tomatoes, sliced in half

½ avocado, sliced into small moons

¼ c pepper jack cheese, hand-shredded

2 T Ken's Buttermilk Ranch Dressing

Directions:

Assemble ingredients by sections.

Cover the entire bottom of the plate with lettuce.

In one corner (relative if you have a round plate) place the tomatoes.

In the opposite section place the avocado strips in a fan shape.

In the third section place the bacon bits.

In the fourth section place the hand-shredded cheese. In the center place the chicken.

Drizzle with the salad dressing and serve.

Freezing Instructions:

The chicken can be frozen in a zip-lock bag. Microwave 1 minute to serve. The salad can be combined in one bowl, or packed in individual containers and placed in the fridge.

Tuna Croquettes

(Total Time: 9 Min|Serves: 4)
Calories: 105g

Total Fat: 5g;

Protein: 14g;

Dietary Fiber: 1g;

Total Carbs: 2g

Sugar: 0;

Sodium: 265mg

Ingredients:

1 can tuna, drained

1 large egg

8 T grated Parmesan cheese

2 T flax meal dash salt dash pepper

1 T minced onion

Directions:

Blend all ingredients except the flax meal

Form into patties (¼ cup ea.)

Dip both sides in the flax meal

Fry until browned on both sides

Freezing Instructions:

Place patties in one zip-lock bag each. Microwave 1 minute to serve.

Tacos

(Total Time: 25 Min|Serves: 3)

Ingredients:

- 2 cups cheddar cheese, grated
- 1 small avocado, pitted, peeled, and chopped
- 1 cup taco meat, cooked
- 2 teaspoons sriracha sauce
- ¼ cup tomatoes, cored and chopped
- Vegetable oil cooking spray
- Salt and ground black pepper, to taste

Directions:

Spray some cooking oil on lined baking dish. Spread the cheddar cheese on the baking sheet, place in an oven at 400°F, and bake for 15 minutes. Spread taco meat over cheese, and bake for 10 minutes. In a bowl, mix the avocado with tomatoes, sriracha sauce, salt, and pepper, and stir. Spread this over the taco and cheddar layers, let the tacos to cool, slice using a pizza cutter, and serve.

Cucumber Soup

(Total Time: 0 Min|Serves: 4)
Calories: 169

Total Fat: 12g;

Protein: 4g;

Total Carbs: 9g

Dietary Fiber: 5g;

Sugar: 6g;

Sodium: 494mg

Ingredients:

2 T minced garlic

4 c English cucumbers, peeled and diced

½ c onion, diced

1 T lemon juice

1 ½ cups chicken broth

½ tsp salt

1 diced avocado

¼ tsp red pepper flakes

¼ cup diced parsley

½ cup Greek yogurt, plain

Directions:

Place all the ingredients and emulsify by blending, except ½ c chopped cucumber.

Blend until smooth.

Pour into 4 servings.

Top with reserved cucumber.

Freezing Instructions:

Freeze in one cup containers with lids. Let thaw to serve or microwave 2 minutes to serve hot.

Dinner

Grilled Chicken Wings

(Total Time: 15 Min|Serves: 5)

Ingredients:

- 2 pounds wings
- Juice of 1 lime
- ½ cup fresh cilantro, chopped
- 2 garlic cloves, peeled and minced
- 1 jalapeño pepper, chopped
- 3 tablespoons coconut oil
- Salt and ground black pepper, to taste
- Lime wedges, for serving
- Ranch dip, for serving

Directions:

In a bowl, mix the lime juice with the cilantro, garlic, jalapeño, coconut oil, salt, and pepper, and whisk. Add the chicken wings, toss to coat, and keep in the refrigerator for 2 hours. Place the chicken wings on a preheated grill over medium-high heat, and cook for 7 minutes on each side. Serve the chicken wings with ranch dip and lime wedges.

Slow-roasted Beef

(Total Time: 480 Min|Serves: 8)

Ingredients:

- 5 pounds beef roast
- Salt and ground black pepper, to taste
- ½ teaspoon celery salt
- 2 teaspoons chili powder
- 1 tablespoon avocado oil
- 1 tablespoon sweet paprika
- A pinch of cayenne pepper
- ½ teaspoon garlic powder
- ½ cup beef stock
- 1 tablespoon garlic, minced
- ¼ teaspoon dry mustard

Directions:

Heat up a pan with the oil over medium-high heat, add the beef roast, and brown it on all sides. In a bowl, mix the paprika with chili powder, celery salt, salt, pepper, cayenne, garlic powder, and dry mustard, and stir. Add the roast, rub well, and transfer it to a slow cooker. Add the beef stock and garlic over roast, and cook on low for 8 hours. Transfer the beef to a cutting board, leave it to cool, slice, and divide between plates. Strain the juices from the pot, drizzle over the meat, and serve.

Roasted Salmon

(Total Time: 12 Min|Serves: 4)
Ingredients:

- 2 tablespoons butter, softened
- 1¼ pound salmon fillet
- 2 ounces kimchi, diced
- Salt and ground black pepper, to taste

Directions:

In a food processor, mix kimchi, and blend well. Rub the salmon with salt, pepper, and kimchi mixture with butter, and place into a baking dish. Place in an oven at 425°F, and bake for 15 minutes. Divide between plates and serve.

Easy Baked Chicken

(Total Time: 20 Min | Serves: 4)

Ingredients:

- 4 bacon strips
- 4 chicken breasts
- 3 green onions, chopped
- 4 ounces ranch dressing
- 1 ounce coconut aminos
- 2 tablespoons coconut oil
- 4 ounces cheddar cheese, grated

Directions:

Heat up a pan with the oil over high heat, add the chicken breasts, cook for 7 minutes, flip, and cook for 7 more minutes. Heat up another pan over medium-high heat, add the bacon, cook until crispy, transfer to paper towels, drain the grease, and crumble. Transfer the chicken breast to a baking dish, add the coconut aminos, crumbled bacon, cheese, and green onions on top, introduce in an oven, set on broiler, and cook at a high temperature for 5 minutes. Divide on plates and serve.

Italian Pork Rolls

(Total Time: 12 Min | Serves: 6)

Ingredients:

- 6 prosciutto slices
- 2 tablespoons fresh parsley, chopped
- 1 pound pork cutlets, sliced thin
- ⅓ cup ricotta cheese
- 1 tablespoon coconut oil
- ¼ cup onion, chopped
- 3 garlic cloves, peeled and minced
- 2 tablespoons Parmesan cheese, grated
- 15 ounces canned diced tomatoes
- ⅓ cup chicken stock
- Salt and ground black pepper, to taste
- ½ teaspoon Italian seasoning

Directions:

Use a meat pounder to flatten the pork pieces. Place the prosciutto slices on top of each piece, then divide the ricotta cheese, parsley, and Parmesan cheese. Roll each pork piece and secure with a toothpick. Heat up a pan with the oil over medium heat, add the pork rolls, cook until they are brown on both sides, and transfer to a plate. Heat up the pan again over medium heat, add the garlic and onion, stir, and cook for 5 minutes. Add the stock and cook for 3 minutes. Discard the toothpicks from pork rolls and return them to the pan. Add the tomatoes, Italian seasoning, salt, and pepper, stir, bring to a boil, reduce heat to medium-low, cover pan, and cook for 30 minutes. Divide between plates and serve.

Lemon and Garlic Pork

(Total Time: 30 Min|Serves: 4)
Ingredients:

- 3 tablespoons butter
- 4 pork steaks, bone-in
- 1 cup chicken stock
- Salt and ground black pepper, to taste
- A pinch of lemon pepper
- 3 tablespoons coconut oil
- 6 garlic cloves, peeled and minced
- 2 tablespoons fresh parsley, chopped
- 8 ounces mushrooms, chopped
- 1 lemon, sliced

Directions:

Heat up a pan with 2 tablespoons butter and 2 tablespoons oil over medium-high heat, add the pork steaks, season with salt and pepper, cook until they are brown on both sides, and transfer to a plate. Return the pan to medium heat, add the rest of the butter, and oil, and half of the stock. Stir well, and cook for 1 minute. Stir, and cook for 4 minutes after adding garlic and mushrooms. Add the lemon slices, the rest of the stock, salt, pepper, and lemon pepper, stir and cook everything for 5 minutes. Return the pork steaks to pan and cook everything for 10 minutes. Divide the steaks and sauce between plates and serve.

Easy Baked Chicken

(Total Time: 20 Min|Serves: 4)

Ingredients:

- 4 bacon strips
- 4 chicken breasts
- 3 green onions, chopped
- 4 ounces ranch dressing
- 1-ounce coconut aminos
- 2 tablespoons coconut oil
- 4 ounces cheddar cheese, grated

Directions:

Heat up a pan with the oil over high heat, add the chicken breasts, cook for 7 minutes, flip, and cook for 7 more minutes. Heat up another pan over medium-high heat, add the bacon, cook until crispy, transfer to paper towels, drain the grease, and crumble. Transfer the chicken breast to a baking dish, add the coconut aminos, crumbled bacon, cheese, and green onions on top, introduce in an oven, set on the broiler, and cook at a high temperature for 5 minutes. Divide between plates and serve.

Lemon Chicken

(Total Time: 45 Min|Serves: 6)

Ingredients:

- 1 whole chicken, cut into medium-sized pieces
- Salt and ground black pepper, to taste
- Juice from 2 lemons
- Zest from 2 lemons
- Lemon rinds from 2 lemons

Directions:

Put the chicken pieces in a baking dish, season with some salt and pepper, and drizzle lemon juice. Toss to coat well, add the lemon zest, and lemon rinds, place in an oven at 375ºF and bake for 45 minutes. Discard the lemon rinds, divide the chicken onto plates, drizzle sauce from the baking dish over it, and serve.

Dessert, Appetizers, Side Dish and Salads

Portobello Mushrooms

(Total Time: 10 Min|Serves: 4)

Ingredients:

- 12 ounces Portobello mushrooms, sliced
- Salt and ground black pepper, to taste
- ½ teaspoon dried basil
- 2 tablespoons olive oil
- ½ teaspoon tarragon, dried
- ½ teaspoon dried rosemary
- ½ teaspoon dried thyme
- 2 tablespoons balsamic vinegar

Directions:

In a bowl, mix the oil with vinegar, salt, pepper, rosemary, tarragon, basil, and thyme, and whisk. Add the mushroom slices, toss to coat well, place them on a preheated grill over medium-high heat, cook for 5 minutes on both sides, and serve.

Avocado Fries

(Total Time: 10 Min|Serves: 3)

Ingredients:

- 3 avocados, pitted, peeled, halved, and sliced
- 1½ cups sunflower oil
- 1½ cups almond meal
- A pinch of cayenne pepper
- Salt and ground black pepper, to taste

Directions:

In a bowl, mix the almond meal with salt, pepper, and cayenne, and stir. In a second bowl, whisk eggs with a pinch of salt, and pepper. Dredge the avocado pieces in egg, and then in almond meal mixture. Heat up a pan with the oil over medium-high heat, add the avocado fries, and cook them until they are golden. Transfer to paper towels, drain grease, and divide on plates and serve.

Mushrooms and Spinach

(Total Time: 10 Min|Serves: 4)

Ingredients:

- 10 ounces spinach leaves, chopped
- Salt and ground black pepper, to taste
- 14 ounces mushrooms, chopped
- 2 garlic cloves, peeled and minced
- ½ cup fresh parsley, chopped
- 1 onion, peeled and chopped
- 4 tablespoons olive oil
- 2 tablespoons balsamic vinegar

Directions:

Heat up a pan with the oil over medium-high heat, add the garlic and onion, stir, and cook for 4 minutes. Add the mushrooms, stir, and cook for 3 minutes. Add the spinach, stir, and cook for 3 minutes. Add the vinegar, salt, and pepper, stir, and cook for 1 minute. Add the parsley, stir, divide on plates, and serve.

Nutty Breakfast Smoothie

(Total Time: 0 Min|Serves: 1)

Ingredients:
- 2 brazil nuts
- 1 cup coconut milk
- 10 almonds
- 2 cups spinach leaves
- 1 teaspoon greens powder
- 1 teaspoon whey protein
- 1 tablespoon psyllium seeds
- 1 tablespoon potato starch

Directions:

In a blender, mix the spinach with Brazil nuts, coconut milk, and almonds and blend well. Add the green powder, whey protein, potato starch, and psyllium seeds, and blend well. Pour into a tall glass and serve.

Cauliflower Mash

(Total Time: 10 Min|Serves: 2)

Ingredients:
- ¼ cup sour cream
- 1 small cauliflower head, separated into florets

- Salt and ground black pepper, to taste
- 2 tablespoons feta cheese, crumbled
- 2 tablespoons black olives, pitted and sliced

Directions:

Put water in a pot, add some salt, bring to a boil over medium heat, add the florets, cook for 10 minutes, take off the heat, and drain. Return the cauliflower to the pot, add salt, black pepper, and sour cream, and blend using an immersion blender. Add the black olives and feta cheese, stir and serve.

Simple Kimchi

(Total Time: 0 Min|Serves: 6)

Ingredients:

- 3 tablespoons salt
- 1 pound napa cabbage, chopped
- 1 carrot, julienned
- ½ cup daikon radish
- 3 green onion stalks, chopped
- 1 tablespoon fish sauce
- 3 tablespoons chili flakes
- 3 garlic cloves, peeled and minced

- 1 tablespoon sesame oil
- ½-inch fresh ginger, peeled and grated

Directions:

In a bowl, mix the cabbage with the salt, massage well for 10 minutes, cover, and set aside for 1 hour. In a bowl, mix the chili flakes with fish sauce, garlic, sesame oil, and ginger, and stir well. Drain the cabbage well, rinse under cold water, and transfer to a bowl. Add the carrots, green onions, radish, and chili paste, and stir. Leave in a dark and cold place for at least 2 days before serving.

Chocolate Bombs

(Total Time: 10 Min|Serves: 12)

Ingredients:

- 10 tablespoons coconut oil
- 3 tablespoons macadamia nuts, chopped
- 2 packets stevia
- 5 tablespoons unsweetened coconut powder
- A pinch of salt

Directions:

Put the coconut oil in a pot and melt over medium heat. Add the stevia, salt, and cocoa powder, stir well, and take off the heat.

Spoon this into a candy tray and keep in the refrigerator for a couple of hours. Sprinkle the macadamia nuts on top, and keep in the refrigerator until ready to serve.

Roasted Cauliflower

(Total Time: 25 Min|Serves: 6)

Ingredients:

- 1 cauliflower head, separated into florets
- Salt and ground black pepper, to taste
- ⅓ cup Parmesan cheese, grated
- 1 tablespoon fresh parsley, chopped
- 3 tablespoons olive oil

- 2 tablespoons extra virgin olive oil

Directions:

In a bowl, mix the oil with garlic, salt, pepper, and cauliflower florets. Toss to coat well, spread this on a lined baking sheet, place in an oven at 450°F, and bake for 25 minutes, stirring halfway. Add the Parmesan cheese, and parsley, stir and cook for 5 minutes. Divide on plates and serve.

Broiled Brussels Sprouts

(Total Time: 10 Min|Serves: 4)

Ingredients:

- 1 pound Brussels sprouts, trimmed and halved
- Salt and ground black pepper, to taste
- 1 teaspoon sesame seeds
- 1 tablespoon green onions, chopped
- 1½ tablespoons sukrin gold syrup
- 1 tablespoon coconut aminos
- 2 tablespoons sesame oil
- 1 tablespoon sriracha

Directions:

In a bowl, mix the sesame oil with coconut aminos, sriracha, syrup, salt, and black pepper, and whisk. Heat up a pan over medium-high heat, add the Brussels sprouts, and cook them for 5 minutes on each side. Add the sesame oil mixture, toss to coat, sprinkle sesame seeds, and green onions, stir again, and serve.

Doughnut

(Total Time: 15 Min | Serves: 24)

Ingredients:

- ¼ cup erythritol
- ¼ cup flaxseed meal
- ¾ cup almond flour
- 1 teaspoon baking powder
- 1 teaspoon vanilla extract
- 2 eggs
- 3 tablespoons coconut oil
- ¼ cup coconut milk
- 20 drops red food coloring
- A pinch of salt
- 1 tablespoon cocoa powder

Directions:

In a bowl, mix the flaxseed meal with almond flour, cocoa powder, baking powder, erythritol, and salt, and stir. In another bowl, mix the coconut oil with coconut milk, vanilla extract, food coloring, and eggs, and stir. Combine the 2 mixtures, stir using a hand mixer, transfer to a bag, make a hole in the bag, and shape 12 doughnuts on a baking sheet. Place in an oven at 350°F, and bake for 15 minutes. Arrange them on a platter and serve.

Oven-fried Green Beans

(Total Time: 10 Min|Serves: 4)

Ingredients:

- ⅔ cup Parmesan cheese, grated
- 1 egg
- 12 ounces green beans
- Salt and ground black pepper, to taste
- ½ teaspoon garlic powder
- ¼ teaspoon paprika

Directions:

In a bowl, mix the Parmesan cheese with salt, pepper, garlic powder, and paprika. In another bowl, whisk the egg with salt and pepper. Dredge the green beans in egg, and then in the Parmesan mixture. Place the green beans on a lined baking sheet, place in an oven at 400°F for 10 minutes. Serve hot.

Pesto

(Total Time: 0 Min|Serves: 4)

Ingredients:

- ½ cup olive oil
- 2 cups basil
- ⅓ cup pine nuts
- ⅓ cup Parmesan cheese, grated
- 2 garlic cloves, peeled and chopped

- Salt and ground black pepper, to taste

Directions:

Put the basil in a food processor, add the pine nuts, and garlic, and blend well. Add the Parmesan cheese, salt, pepper, and the oil gradually and blend again until you obtain a paste. Serve with chicken or vegetables.

Creamy Spinach

(Total Time: 15 Min | Serves: 2)

Ingredients:

- 2 garlic cloves, peeled and minced
- 8 ounces spinach leaves
- A drizzle of olive oil
- Salt and ground black pepper, to taste
- 4 tablespoons sour cream
- 1 tablespoon butter
- 2 tablespoons Parmesan cheese, grated

Directions:

Heat up a pan with the oil over medium heat, add the spinach, stir and cook until it softens. Add the salt, pepper, butter, Parmesan cheese, and butter, stir, and cook for 4 minutes. Add the sour cream, stir, and cook for 5 minutes. Divide on plates and serve.

Bonus Recipes

Artichoke Frittata

(Serves: 4 Time: 15 Minutes)

Calories: 199

Protein: 16 Grams

Fat: 13 Grams

Carbs: 5 Grams

Ingredients:

- 8 Eggs, Large
- ¼ Cup Asiago Cheese, Grated
- 1 Tablespoon Basil, Fresh & Chopped
- 1 Teaspoon Oregano, Fresh & Chopped
- ¼ Teaspoon Sea Salt, Fine
- ¼ Teaspoon Black Pepper
- 1 Teaspoon Olive Oil
- 1 Teaspoon Garlic, Minced
- 1 Can Water Packed Artichoke Hearts, Quartered & Drained
- 1 Tomato, Chopped

Directions:

1. Start by heating your oven to a broil, and then get out a bowl. Whisk your asiago cheese, basil, oregano, eggs, pepper and salt together. Make sure it's well blended, and then get out a skillet that's ovenproof.

Place it over medium-high heat, and heat up your olive oil. Add in your garlic and sauté for a minute.
2. Remove it from the skillet, and then heat and pour in your egg mixture. Return the skillet to heat before sprinkling in your tomato and artichoke hearts.
3. Cook without stirring for eight minutes. The center should set. Place your skillet in the oven, and broil for a minute. The top should be puffed and lightly brown.
4. Serve warm.

Vegetarian Lasagna

(Serves: 6 Time: 1 Hour 15 Minutes)

Calories: 386

Protein: 15 Grams

Fat: 11 Grams

Carbs: 59 Grams

Ingredients:

- 1 Sweet Onion, Sliced Thick
- 1 Eggplant, Sliced Thick
- 2 Zucchini, Sliced Lengthwise
- 2 Tablespoons Olive Oil
- 28 Ounces Canned tomatoes, Diced & Sodium Free
- 1 Cup Quartered, Canned & Water Packed Artichokes, Drained
- 2 Teaspoons Basil, Fresh & Chopped
- 2 Teaspoons Garlic, Minced
- 2 Teaspoons Oregano, Fresh & Chopped
- 12 Lasagna Noodles, Whole Grain & No Boil
- ¼ Teaspoon Red Pepper Flakes
- ¾ Cup Asiago Cheese, Grated

Directions:

1. Start by heating your oven to 400, and then get out a baking sheet. Line it with foil before placing it to the side.
2. Get out a large bowl and toss your zucchini, yellow squash, eggplant, onion and olive oil, making sure it's coated well.
3. Arrange your vegetables on the baking sheet, roasting for twenty minutes. They should be lightly caramelized and tender.
4. Chop your roasted vegetables before placing them in a bowl.

5. Stir in your garlic, basil, oregano, artichoke hearts, tomatoes and red pepper flakes, spooning a quarter of this mixture in the bottom of a nine by thirteen baking dish. Arrange four lasagna noodles over this sauce, and continue by alternating it. Sprinkle with asiago cheese on top, baking for a half hour.
6. Slice to serve after cooling.

Chicken & Vegetable Wraps

(Serves: 4 Time: 15 Minutes)

Calories: 278

Protein: 27 Grams

Fat: 7 Grams

Carbs: 28 Grams

Ingredients:

- ¼ Cup Greek Yogurt, Plain
- 2 Cups Chicken, Cooked & Chopped
- ½ Red Bell Pepper, Diced
- ½ English Cucumber, Diced
- ½ Cup Carrot, Shredded
- 1 Scallion, Chopped
- ½ Teaspoon Thyme, Fresh & Chopped
- 1 Tablespoon Lemon Juice, Fresh
- 4 Tortillas, Multigrain
- ¼ Teaspoon Sea Salt, Fine
- ¼ Teaspoon Black Pepper

Directions:

1. Start by getting out a bowl and mix your cucumber, red bell pepper, chicken, scallion, carrot, lemon juice, thyme, yogurt, sea salt and pepper. Mix well.

2. Spoon a quarter of this mixture into each tortilla, folding it over to make a pocket. Repeat with your remaining ingredients.

Scallops in a Citrus Sauce

(Serves: 4 Time: 25 Minutes)

Calories: 207

Protein: 26 Grams

Fat: 4 Grams

Carbs: 17 Grams

Ingredients:

- 2 Teaspoons Olive Oil
- 1 Shallot, Minced
- 20 Sea Scallops, Cleaned
- 1 Teaspoon Lime Zest
- 1 Tablespoon Lemon Zest
- 2 Teaspoons Orange Zest
- 1 Tablespoon Basil, Fresh & Chopped
- ½ Cup Orange Juice, Fresh
- 2 Tablespoons Lemon Juice, Fresh
- 2 Tablespoons Honey, Raw

- 1 Tablespoon Greek Yogurt, Plain
- ½ Teaspoon Sea Salt, Fine

Directions:

1. Get out a large skillet and heat up your olive oil over medium-high heat. Add in your shallot, and sauté for a minute. They should soften.
2. Add your scallops in, searing for five minutes. Turn once during this time. They should be tender.
3. Push your scallops to the edge of the skillet, stirring in your three zests, basil, lemon juice and orange juice. Simmer for three minutes.
4. Whisk in your yogurt, honey and sea salt. Cook for four minutes. Coat your scallops in the sauce before serving warm.

Sun Dried Tomato Quiche

(Serves: 4 Time: 40 Minutes)

Calories: 171

Protein: 13 Grams

Fat: 11 Grams

Carbs: 5 Grams

Ingredients:

- 6 Eggs, Large
- ¼ Cup Goat Cheese
- 1/8 Teaspoon Cayenne Pepper
- 2 Tablespoons Milk

- 2 Shallots, Chopped Fine
- 1 Teaspoon Olive Oil
- ½ Teaspoon Garlic, Minced
- 1 Teaspoon Parsley, Fresh & Chopped
- ¼ Teaspoon Sea Salt, Fine
- ¼ Teaspoon Black Pepper
- 10 Sun Dried Tomatoes, Quartered

Directions:

1. Whisk your goat cheese, milk, cayenne and eggs together until they're well blended.
2. Get out an ovenproof skillet that's nine inches, and place it over medium-high heat. Add in your olive oil.
3. Once your olive oil is hot add in your garlic and shallots, and sauté for two minutes. They should be tender and fragrant.
4. Pour your egg mix in, and then scatter your sun dried tomatoes and parsley on top.
5. Season with salt and pepper, and cook it while lifting the edges so that the uncooked egg flows underneath. It will take about three minutes for the bottom to firm.
6. Put your skillet in the oven, and bake for twenty minutes. It should be golden, puffy and the egg should be cooked all the way through.

Asparagus & Kale Pesto Pasta

(Serves: 6 Time: 20 Minutes)

Calories: 283

Protein: 10 Grams

Fat: 12 Grams

Carbs: 33 Grams

Ingredients:

- ¼ Cup Basil, Fresh
- ¾ lb. Asparagus, Trimmed & Chopped Roughly
- ¼ lb. Kale, Washed
- ½ Cup Asiago Cheese, Grated
- ¼ Cup Olive Oil
- 1 Lemon, Juiced & Zested
- ¼ Teaspoon Sea Salt, Fine
- ¼ Teaspoon Black Pepper
- 1 lb. Angel Hair Pasta

Directions:

1. Start by pulsing your kale and asparagus in a food processor until it's finely chopped. Add in your olive oil, lemon juice, basil, and asiago cheese. Continue to pulse until it forms a pesto that's smooth, seasoning with salt and pepper.
2. Cook your pasta according to package instructions before draining it and placing it in a bowl.
3. Add in your pesto and make sure to toss to coat. Sprinkle with lemon zest before serving.

Pork Chops & Peaches

(Serves: 4 Time: 45 Minutes)

Calories; 307

Protein: 38 Grams

Fat: 12 Grams

Carbs: 10 Grams

Ingredients:

- ½ Fennel Bulb, Chopped in 1 Inch Chunks
- 4 Pork Chops, Boneless, 5 Ounces Each & Trimmed
- 2 Tablespoons Olive Oil, Divided + More for Greasing
- 2 Peaches, Pitted & Quartered
- 1 Sweet Onion, Peeled & Sliced Thin
- 2 Tablespoons Balsamic Vinegar
- 1 Teaspoon Thyme, Fresh & Chopped
- 1/4 Teaspoon Sea Salt, Fine
- ¼ Teaspoon Black Pepper

Directions:

1. Heat your oven to 400, and then get out a nine by thirteen inch baking dish. Make sure to grease it with olive oil before placing it to the side. Season your pork chops with salt and pepper.
2. Get out a bowl and toss your onion, peaches, fennel, thyme, balsamic vinegar, a tablespoon of olive oil and thyme. Roast them in your baking dish for twenty minutes.

3. Get out a skillet, placing it over medium-high heat, and heat up your remaining oil.
4. Add in your pork chops, searing for two minutes per side.
5. Take your vegetables out of the oven and stir them. Place the pork chops on top, and then roast for another ten minutes. Your pork should be cooked all the way through.

Mushroom Risotto

(Serves: 4 Time: 40 Minutes)

Calories: 322

Protein: 14 Grams

Fat: 11 Grams

Carbs: 38 Grams

Ingredients:

- 2 Tablespoons Olive Oil
- 1 Shallot, Sliced Thin
- 10 Mushrooms, Large & Sliced
- ½ Cup Red Wine
- 1 Cup Faro
- ½ Cup Vegetable Broth
- ½ Cup Parmesan Cheese
- 1 Tablespoon Flatleaf Parsley, Fresh & Chopped
- ¼ Teaspoon Black Pepper
- 1 Teaspoon Sea Salt, Fine

Directions:

1. Place a skillet over high heat, adding in your shallot and olive oil. Cook for three to five minutes. It should soften, and then add in your red wine and mushrooms. Cook until the wine has evaporated.
2. Add in your faro, cooking for three minutes. Coat it, and then add in ½ cup broth. Stir occasionally while cooking. Your broth should be absorbed, and then add another half a cup. Continue to repeat, and the faro should be tender but not mushy.
3. Turn the heat off, adding in your parsley, salt, pepper and parmesan. Serve warm.

Conclusion

Like every other good thing in life, we have now arrived at the end of this book, but the beginning of your new journey. It is in my sincerest hope that you have learned the fundamentals of meal prepping, along with some recipes that will make a new adventure easy and fun. I have tried my very best here to provide not only the simplest of methods to prepare for meal prep but the most delicious as well.

Please remember that to reach any worthwhile goal in life requires dedication and focus. Remember why you're doing all this, have a strategic plan in place, and discipline yourself to follow through day in and day out. Once you reach the other side of your goal, you'll look back and say it was worth it.

Lastly, I'd like to once again thank you from the bottom of my heart, for choosing my book and I hope it becomes a difference maker in your life.

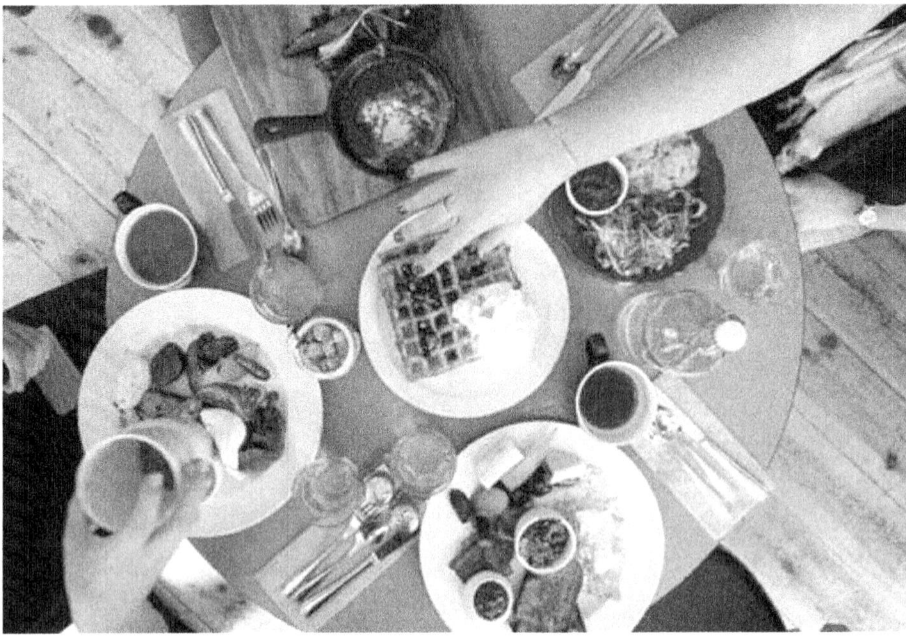

Printed in Great Britain
by Amazon